D1029198

THE ISENBERG MEMORIAL
LECTURE SERIES
1965–1966

THE ISENBERG MEMORIAL LECTURE SERIES 1965–1966

Carl G. Hempel   *Henry David Aiken*

W. V. Quine   *John Wild*

J. O. Urmson   *Aron Gurwitsch*

Stuart Hampshire   *Quentin Lauer, S. J.*

Walter Kaufmann

THE

MICHIGAN STATE UNIVERSITY PRESS

1969

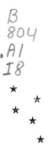

CONTENTS

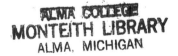

INTRODUCTORY NOTE

THE ANNUAL ISENBERG MEMORIAL Lecture Series began in the fall of 1965. Each year since then outstanding philosophers have come to the Michigan State University campus to deliver a public address (in a designated general area) and hold one or two seminars with interested faculty and students. The Series has become one of the most distinguished of its type in America.

The present volume consists of papers based on most of the lectures given in 1965–66.[1] It is dedicated to the memory of Arnold Isenberg, a former teacher, then friend and colleague at Michigan State, whose sudden death at the age of fifty-three, on February 26, 1965, shocked and saddened those who knew him.

Arnold Isenberg received the degrees of A.B., A.M., and Ph.D. at Harvard during the early thirties. In June, 1962, after teaching philosophy at Cornell University, Harvard, Queens College and Stanford, he joined the Michigan State University

---

1. Professor Adolph Grünbaum's paper, "Modern Science and Zeno's Paradoxes of Motion," has been published elsewhere.

faculty. He was editor of *John Dewey: Theory of the Moral Life* (1960), and co-editor of *Aesthetic Theories* (1964). But the philosophical world will probably remember him chiefly for his many fine articles, especially in the field of aesthetics where he made a distinctive contribution. His "Critical Communication" (1949) and "Perception, Meaning, and the Subject-Matter of Art" (1944) are but two examples. These papers are brilliantly written, insightful, and display a very subtle analytical approach. It is thus fitting that his name should have been given to this series.

The present collection is divided into three parts, each representing a topic dealt with during one of the three terms of the academic year 1965–66. The Fall Term topic was "The Philosophy of Science." Carl Gustav Hempel, the first contributor in the series, was trained originally in science, receiving his Ph.D. from Berlin in 1934. Later he was a member of the so-called Berlin Group. He left Germany in the thirties, and has taught philosophy at Princeton for many years since then. His publications include "Problems and Changes in the Empiricist Criterion of Meaning" (1950), *Fundamentals of Concept Formation in Empirical Science* (1952), "A Purely Syntactical Definition of Confirmation" (1943), "Studies in the Logic of Confirmation" (1945), "A Definition of 'Degree of Confirmation'" (1945, with P. Oppenheim), "Studies in the Logic of Explanation" (1948, with P. Oppenheim), and "Deductive-Nomological vs. Statistical Explanation" (1962).

Willard van Orman Quine, the second contributor, received his undergraduate training at Oberlin. He wrote his doctoral dissertation under Whitehead at Harvard, where he is now Edgar Pierce Professor of Philosophy. Like Hempel, his influence in the field of philosophy has been considerable. The following are some of his more important publications: "Two Dogmas of Empiricism" (1951), "On What There Is" (1948), *Word and Object* (1960), "Mr. Strawson on Logical Theory" (1953), "Truth by Convention" (1936), and "Steps

Toward a Constructive Nominalism" (1947, with Nelson Goodman).

The topic for the Winter Term was "Value Theory and Analytic Philosophy." Two of the philosophers represented here were drawn from universities in Great Britain. J. O. Urmson is Fellow and Tutor in Philosophy, Corpus Christi College, Oxford, and was Visiting Professor in the University of Michigan, 1965–66. His publications include *Philosophical Analysis* (1956), and contributions to *Logic and Language* (1953), *Essays in Conceptual Analysis* (1956), *Essays in Moral Philosophy* (1958). He is editor of *The Concise Encyclopedia of Western Philosophy and Philosophers.*

Stuart Hampshire was also educated, and subsequently taught philosophy, at Oxford. Later he became Grote Professor of Philosophy of Mind and Logic at the University of London. Since 1963 he has been teaching philosophy at Princeton. His writings include *Spinoza* (1951), *The Age of Reason* (1956), *Thought and Action* (1959).

The third contributor to "Value Theory and Analytic Philosophy" was American-born Henry D. Aiken. After studying at Reed College and Stanford, he went to Harvard, where he received his Ph.D. in 1943. He has taught philosophy at Harvard, Columbia, and the University of Washington. Presently he is Professor of Philosophy at Brandeis University. He has published *The Age of Ideology* (1957), *Reason and Conduct* (1962), and contributed to anthologies and philosophical journals.

The topic in the Spring Term was "Phenomenology and Existentialism." John Wild, the first lecturer, was educated at Harvard and the University of Chicago, where he received his Ph.D. in 1926. In 1963, after teaching philosophy at Harvard and Northwestern, he went to Yale. His publications include *Plato's Modern Enemies and the Theory of Natural Law* (1953), *Challenge of Existentialism* (1955), and *Existence and the World of Freedom* (1963).

Aron Gurwitsch was educated at the Universities of Berlin

and Frankfurt, receiving his Ph.D. from the University of
Göttingen in 1929. During the thirties he lectured in philosophy at the Sorbonne. In the forties he held various academic
appointments at John Hopkins, Harvard, Wheaton College,
and Brandeis University. Presently he is Professor of Philosophy at the New School for Social Research. He has published
*Field of Consciousness, Studies in Phenomenology and Psy-
chology* (1966), as well as numerous articles.

The Reverend (Joseph) Quentin Lauer, S.J. received the
degrees of B.A., Ph.L. and M.A. from St. Louis University;
St. T.L., from Woodstock College; and D. ès L., from the University of Paris in 1955. Since 1954 he has been a member of
the faculty of Fordham University. In addition to articles in
various journals, his publications include *Phénoménologie de
Husserl* (1955). The original title of the English paperback
was *The Triumph of Subjectivity* (1958).

Walter Kaufmann, the final Isenberg speaker in the Spring
Term, attended Williams College and Harvard, where he received his Ph.D. in 1947. The same year he began teaching
at Princeton, where he is presently Professor of Philosophy. He
has also taught at Cornell University, the New School for
Social Research, Columbia University, University of Washington, American University, University of Michigan, Brooklyn
College, Frankfurt, Germany, and at the Hebrew University
in Jerusalem. His many publications include *Nietzsche*
(1950), *Critique of Religion and Philosophy* (1958) and
From Shakespeare to Existentialism (1959).

Here, then, is a collection of papers by nine distinguished
men with quite diverse backgrounds and interests. The present
volume should be of interest to the scholar as well to the
general reader interested in contemporary philosophy. The
papers are not intended to teach philosophy, but rather to
give some idea of what is going on in the field.

Ronald Suter
East Lansing, Michigan

Carl G. Hempel

ON THE STRUCTURE

OF

SCIENTIFIC THEORIES

1. TWO SCHEMATIC CONSTRUALS OF A THEORY.

The questions to be examined in this essay concern, broadly speaking, the logical structure and the epistemic status of scientific theories. To a large extent, my discussion will deal with the well-known conception of a theory as consisting of, or being decomposable into, two principal components:

(1) An uninterpreted deductive system, usually thought of as an axiomatized calculus C, whose postulates correspond to the basic principles of the theory and provide implicit definitions for its constitutive terms;

(2) A set R of statements that assign empirical meaning to the terms and the sentences of C by linking them to potential observational or experimental findings and thus interpreting them, ultimately, in terms of some observational vocabulary. Such statements, conceived as subject to more or less stringent syntactic and semantic requirements, have been variously referred to as the entries of a "dictionary" for translating theoretical into experimental language, as "rules of cor-

respondence" or "rules of interpretation", as "coordinating definitions" and, of course, as "operational definitions".

Some writers have put considerable emphasis on the need for a third constituent of a good scientific theory, namely a model (in an appropriate sense of the word) which interprets the abstract calculus C in terms of concepts or principles with which we are acquainted by previous experience. This point is not of immediate relevance to the issues with which I propose to deal first; it will, however, be considered later on.

The conception of a theory as consisting of an abstract calculus C and a set R of rules of correspondence will be briefly represented by the following schema, which construes a theory as the sum of two classes of sentences:

(Schema I) $T = C \cup R$

I have myself repeatedly used a construal of this kind in discussing the status of theories and of theoretical entities; but it seems to me now that, while not strictly untenable, it is misleading in several respects. I will point out what seem to me the inadequacies of Schema I by contrasting it with an alternative construal.

As a rule, theories are introduced in a field of scientific inquiry after prior research has yielded a body of initial knowledge—usually in the form of general laws or empirical generalizations—concerning the phenomena under investigation. Theories are then developed in an effort to achieve a deeper and more comprehensive understanding of those phenomena by presenting them as manifestations or resultants of certain underlying processes, and by exhibiting the previously established laws or generalizations as consequences (more accurately: as approximations of consequences) of certain basic general principles assumed to govern the underlying occurrences. This broad characterization applies equally, I think, to the two types of theory which Nagel, following Rankine, distinguishes in his penetrating study of the subject; [1] namely, "abstractive" theories, such as the Newtonian theory of gravitation and motion, and "hypothetical" theories, such as the kinetic theory of heat or the undulatory and corpuscular theories of light.

Prima facie, therefore, it seems reasonable to think of a theory as consisting of statements, or principles, of two kinds; let us call them *internal principles* and *bridge principles* for short. The internal principles will specify the "theoretical scenario"; they will characterize the basic processes posited by the theory, the kinds of entities they involve, and the laws to which they are held to conform. The bridge principles will indicate the ways in which the processes envisaged by the theory are related to the previously investigated empirical phenomena which the theory is intended to explain.

This conception will be indicated by the following schema:

(Schema II) $$T = I \underline{\cup} B$$

Here, I is the class of internal principles, B the class of bridge principles.

There are obvious similarities to the conception indicated by Schema I, but there are also considerable differences; this will become clear in the following amplification and comparison of the two construals.

2. INTERNAL AND BRIDGE PRINCIPLES; THEORETICAL AND PRE-THEORETICAL TERMS.

Consider first the vocabularies (apart from logical and mathematical terms) in which the two sets of principles, I and

---

1. E. Nagel, *The Structure of Science;* New York: Harcourt, Brace and World, Inc., 1961; pp. 125–129.

B, are expressed. The formulation of the internal principles will normally make use of a "theoretical vocabulary"; V_T, i.e., a set of terms introduced specifically to characterize the various constituents of the theoretical scenario and the laws assumed to govern them. The formulation of the bridge principles will require, in addition to the theoretical vocabulary, a set of terms suited to describe the empirical phenomena and uniformities that the theory is intended to explain. The terms of this second kind are therefore available and understood prior to the formulation of the theory; they may therefore be said to constitute, relative to the theory in question, an antecedently understood, or pre-theoretical, vocabulary V_A. For the terms of this vocabulary, there are objective rules of use which, at least initially, are independent of the theory. A vocabulary of this kind is equally presupposed, of course, by the conception of correspondence rules invoked in Schema I, for those rules are assumed to impart empirical meanings upon certain expressions of the calculus C by linking them to an appropriate experimental or observational subject matter.

Thus, the pre-theoretical vocabulary has often been construed as consisting of observational terms. Broadly speaking, an observational term is one that stands for some characteristic of things or events that is directly observable, i.e., whose presence or absence in a particular case can, under suitable circumstances (such as normal lighting or the like), be ascertained by direct observation, without the use of special instruments. Thus, such words as 'blue', 'liquid', 'hot', 'acrid-smelling', 'longer than', 'contiguous with', might count as observational terms.

Closer studies of this idea strongly suggest, however, that the usual characterizations of observability fall short of determining a sufficiently clear and analytically useful dividing line between observational and nonobservational terms. It could be argued, for example, that under the rough criterion just mentioned, such terms as 'electrically charged', 'acid', and 'has a higher refractive index than' qualify as observational, since for each of them, circumstances can be specified in which the presence or absence of the characteristic in question can be ascertained very reliably by means of a few direct observations.[2]

The notion of observability presents another puzzling aspect, which does not seem to have been widely noticed, and which therefore might deserve brief mention here. The distinction between "directly observable" and "not directly observable" has been applied by many of its proponents not only to attributes (i.e., properties and relations) of physical objects and processes, but also to those objects and processes themselves. Thus, such things as mountains, chairs, and apples are said to be directly observable; electrons, photons, and mesons are not. Similarly, events or processes such as a thunderstorm or the motion of a car might be said to be observable, whereas quantum jumps or the mutual annihilation of a particle and a corresponding antiparticle might be qualified as not directly observable. But is the notion of observability as invoked in these contexts identical with that applied to attributes, or can it at least be explicated in terms of the latter? For brevity, I will limit my comments on this question to the case of "thing-like" entities; they can readily be extended to processes and events.

As is illustrated by the example of mountains, chairs, electrons, mesons, and the like, thing-like entities are often referred to by means of descriptive predicate terms. Now, under the rough criterion stated above, predicates like 'chair' (or 'is a chair'), 'mountain', and 'apple' would count as observational, whereas predicates like 'electron', 'meson', and 'photon' would

2. For a discussion of some of the difficulties besetting the distinction between observational and theoretical terms, and for further bibliographic references, see, for example, H. Putnam, "What Theories are Not"; in E. Nagel, P. Suppes, A. Tarski (eds.), *Logic, Methodology and Philosophy of Science;* Stanford: Stanford University Press, 1962; pp. 240–251; and P. Achinstein, "The Problem of Theoretical Terms", *American Philosophical Quarterly* 2, 193–203. (1965).

not. Hence it might seem that observability for thing-like entities can be explicated as follows in terms of observability for attributes of things: When '*P*' is a predicate term, then the entities describable as *P*'s are observable if and only if '*P*' is an observational predicate. Thus, apples are observable, and indeed the word 'apple' is an observational predicate; it stands for a directly observable characteristic of physical bodies. And mesons are non-observable; and indeed, the word 'meson' is not an observational predicate.

But the proposed explication is quite incorrect. Consider such entities as diamonds, Stradivarius violins, precision chronometers, purebred Pekinese dogs, or philosophers. All of them are objects that can be directly seen, felt, and in most cases also heard—in contrast to electrons and the like, which can not. Yet the expressions 'diamond', 'Stradivarius violin', 'precision chronometer', 'purebred Pekinese' and 'philosopher' are none of them observational predicates: The presence or absence of the characteristics they stand for cannot be ascertained by direct observation. Hence it is not the case that objects of kind *P*, or *P*'s for short, are observable if and only if '*P*' is an observational predicate: it may be that *P*'s are observable, but not *qua P*'s, not under that description.

The following alternative explication may appear plausible: An object is directly observable just in case it has at least one directly observable attribute. Thus, Pekinese dogs are furry; Stradivarius violins, like other violins, are hard objects with smooth surfaces of reddish-brown color; and so forth. But the contemplated criterion is too inclusive: an object—a flea's egg, perhaps—may be too small to be directly observable, and may yet have a certain color, say brown, which is observable in the sense that under suitable circumstances—namely, when it occurs on a large enough surface and in natural light—its presence can be quite reliably ascertained by direct observation.

At present, I am unable to offer a satisfactory explication of the concept of observability referring to thing-like entities in terms of the concept of observability as applied to attributes; and the point of the preceding remarks is mainly to note that if in the characterization of theories one wished to make use of the notion of observability, one would presumably need two concepts, both of which are rather vague.

Fortunately, however, the notion of observability is not required for our purposes; for the elements of the pre-theoretical vocabulary V_A need not, and indeed should not, generally be conceived as observational terms in the sense adumbrated above: in many cases, V_A will contain terms originally introduced by an earlier theory that is empirically well supported, and whose internal and bridge principles provide rules for their use. Consider some examples.

In the classical kinetic theory of gases, the internal principles are assumptions about the gas molecules; they concern their size, their mass, their number; and they include also various laws, partly taken over from classical mechanics, partly statistical in nature, pertaining to the motions and collisions of the molecules, and to the resulting changes in their momenta and energies. The bridge principles include statements such as that the temperature of a gas is proportional to to the mean kinetic energy of its molecules, and that the rates at which different gases diffuse through the walls of a container are proportional to the numbers of molecules of the gases in question, and to their average speeds. By means of such bridge principles, certain micro-characteristics of a gas, which belong to the scenario of the kinetic theory, are linked to macroscopic features such as temperature, pressure, and diffusion rate; these can be described, and generalizations concerning them can be formulated, in terms of an antecedently available vocabulary, namely, that of classical thermodynamics. And some of the macroscopic features in question might perhaps be regarded as fairly directly observable or measurable (although, of course, the relevant measurements will require the use of instruments).

But the features to which certain aspects of the theoretical scenario are linked by the bridge principles are not always as close to observability as the volume, temperature, and pressure of a body of gas. Consider, for example, the explanation provided by Bohr's model of the hydrogen atom for the fact that the light emitted by glowing hydrogen vapor is restricted to certain discrete wavelengths, which appear in the hydrogen spectrum as a corresponding set of lines. According to Bohr's model, the hydrogen atom contains one electron, which circles the nucleus in one or another of a series of discrete orbits that are available to it. When a mass of hydrogen gas is electrically or thermally excited, the electrons in some of the atoms are shifted to outer orbits, which represent higher energy states. Eventually, such electrons will jump back from some outer to some inner orbit; in the process, they emit monochromatic radiation whose wave length is uniquely determined by the released energy, which in turn is fully determined by the two orbits between which the jump takes place. Consequently, the radiation emitted by excited hydrogen vapor can assume only certain specific and discrete wave lengths. Moreover, the quantitative details of Bohr's model account for the specific wave lengths associated with the lines in the hydrogen spectrum. In particular, they imply Balmer's formula, an ingenious empirical generalization, which had been previously established, and which specifies the wave lengths of one series of discrete lines, called the Balmer series, in the hydrogen spectrum:

$$\lambda = b \frac{n^2}{n^2 - 4}$$

Here, b is a numerically specified constant; and if n is given the values 3, 4, 5, . . . , the resulting values of λ give the wave lengths of the lines in the Balmer series.

In this case, the internal principles comprise the various assumptions that characterize Bohr's model of the hydrogen atom. The bridge principles, on the other hand, include such statements as these:

(a)   the light emitted by excited hydrogen vapor results from the energy released when electrons jump from outer to inner orbits;

(b)   An electronic jump that releases the energy E results in the emission of light with the wave length

$$\lambda = (h \cdot c) \,/\, E$$

where h is Planck's constant and c the velocity of light.

These and other bridge principles connect the entities and processes posited by the theory with certain features of the subject matter to be explained, namely, the wavelengths associated with the lines in the hydrogen spectrum. But while the lines, and the discrete patterns they form, might be counted as observables, the wave lengths and the corresponding frequencies surely can not; and the terms that serve to characterize them are not observational terms. But they are antecedently understood nonetheless: when Bohr proposed his model, rules for their use, including principles for the measurement of wave lengths, had already been established: these were based on antecedent theories, especially wave optics.

In characterizing scientific theories, it is not necessary, therefore, to presuppose one partition of all scientific terms into observational and theoretical ones. It suffices to note that whatever characteristic terms a new theory introduces will have to be linked by bridge principles to an antecedently understood vocabulary that serves to describe, and to express generalizations about, the subject matter that the theory is to explain.

This observation marks no great departure from the ideas embodied in Schema I; for while the rules of correspondence, R, are often said to connect theoretical terms with observational ones, several writers who have made expository use of that schema have clearly envisaged a less stringent conception that is quite compatible with the one just outlined.

3. ON THE NOTION OF AN AXIOMATIZED THEORETICAL CALCULUS.

But Schema I presents more serious problems. One of them concerns the rationale of dividing a theory into an axiomatized uninterpreted calculus and a set of correspondence rules. Before indicating the difficulties I find with this conception, I want to mention one objection to it that I do not think pertinent. This is the observation that the proposed division into calculus and interpretation has no counterpart in the ways in which theories are actually formulated and used by scientists, and that, moreover, a rigid system *C* can represent at best one momentary stage of what is in fact a continually developing and changing system of ideas. This objection seems to me to miss its mark. For Schema I is meant to reflect certain logical and epistemological features of scientific theories rather than the heuristic and pragmatic aspects of their formulation and use, however interesting and important these may be in their own right.

But this remark immediately raises the question: What are the logical or epistemological characteristics of theories that are pointed up or illuminated by a construal in the manner of Schema I? Consider first the system *C*, which seems clearly intended to include those sentences which, in Schema II, are referred to as the internal principles. This system is conceived, in Schema I, as an axiomatized and uninterpreted calculus. Let us examine the significance of these two characteristics in turn.

As for axiomatization, its great importance in logic and mathematics and their meta-disciplines need not be emphasized here. Under certain conditions, it can undoubtedly provide also philosophical illumination for questions concerning scientific theories; but several among the extant axiomatizations of such theories seem to me to have very little significance either

for the concerns of empirical science or for those of philosophy
—however ingenious they may be as logical accomplishments.

One outstanding example of a philosophically illuminating
use of axiomatization is Reichenbach's work on the philosophical significance of relativistic physics; and his division of
physical geometry into an axiomatized mathematical system
and a set of "coordinative definitions" is an early instance of
a construal of a scientific theory in the manner of Schema I.[3]
While technically inferior to more recent examples, Reichenbach's axiomatization of the relativistic theory of space-time is
distinguished by aiming at definite philosophical objectives:
among other things, it was meant to separate what Reichenbach regarded as conventional or stipulative truths from empirical hypotheses, and more generally, it was to provide a
basis for a critique of Kant's conception of synthetic *a priori*
knowledge.

But while axiomatization, if appropriately used, may be
helpful, it is not necessary for this purpose—nor is it sufficient.
For axiomatization is basically an expository device; it exhibits
logical relationships between statements, but not their epistemic grounds or connections. A given scientific theory admits
of many different axiomatizations, and the postulates chosen in
a particular axiomatization need not, therefore, correspond to
what in some more substantial sense might count as the basic
assumptions of the theory; nor need the terms chosen as un-
defined, or primitive, in a given axiomatization represent what
on epistemological or other grounds might qualify as the basic
concepts of the theory; nor need the formal definitions of other
theoretical terms by means of the chosen primitives correspond to statements which in science would be regarded as
definitionally true and thus analytic. In an axiomatization of

---

3. The axiomatization is given in H. Reichenbach, *Axiomatik der relativistischen Raum-Zeit-Lehre*. Braunschweig: Vieweg, 1924. This book forms the basis of many of the ideas developed in Reichenbach's *Philosophy of Space and Time;* New York: Dover Publications, 1958.

Newtonian mechanics, the second law of motion can be given
the status of a definition, a postulate, or a theorem, as one
pleases; but the rôle it is thus assigned within the axiomatized
system does not indicate whether in its scientific use it functions as a definitional truth, as a basic theoretical law, or as a
derivative one (if indeed it may be said to have just one of
these functions).

Hence, whatever philosophical insights may be obtainable
by considering a theory in an axiomatized form will require
certain appropriate specific axiomatizations and not just any
axiomatization; let alone simply the assumption that the theory
has been put into some unspecified axiomatic form. But this
last assumption alone enters into Schema I, and I do not see
what philosophical illumination it could provide.

4. THE ROLE OF PRE-THEORETICAL CONCEPTS
IN INTERNAL PRINCIPLES.

The system C envisaged in Schema I is, moreover, conceived as uninterpreted in the sense that, within C, the extralogical terms have been assigned no meanings other than those
accruing to them by reason of their role in the postulates,
which thus constitute incomplete "implicit definitions" of the
terms. One root of this idea is doubtless the realization that
the description of the theoretical scenario of a theory normally
makes use of characteristic new terms, which acquire empirical significance and applicability only when they are suitably
linked to pre-theoretical terms, antecedently used in the field
of inquiry. But the conception of C as an uninterpreted system
suggests that the internal principles of a theory are formulated
exclusively in terms of the "new" theoretical vocabulary V_T
(plus logical and mathematical symbols), which logically play
the rôle of variables or dummies. All the sentences of C would
then have the character of schemata such as these: 'All X's

are Y's or Z's'; 'Every Y has three quantitative characteristics, q, r, s, such that $q = c \cdot r \cdot s$, where c is a constant', and so forth.[4] Actually, however, the internal principles of most, if not all, scientific theories contain not only the terms of the theoretical vocabulary; but also pre-theoretical terms, taken over from the antecedently available vocabulary. To state the point more intuitively: The theoretical scenario is normally described to a large extent by means of terms which already have definite empirical content, and which are already understood, prior to, and independently of, the theory. For example, the theoretical assumptions of the classical kinetic theory of gases attribute masses, volumes, velocities, momenta, kinetic energies, and other characteristics familiar from the study of macroscopic objects, to molecules and to atoms; and the classical wave and particle theories of light characterize the processes in their theoretical scenarios by means of the concepts of wave length, frequency, velocity of a wave; path of a particle; deflection of a particle as a result of attraction—all of which are antecedently understood.

Hence, the internal principles of a theory, and thus, the system C, must be viewed as containing two kinds of extralogical terms, as indicated by the following schematization:

$$I = \Phi \ (t_1, t_2, \ \ldots t_k; p_1, p_2, \ \ldots, p_m)$$

Here, the t's are terms belonging to the theoretical vocabulary of T, whereas the p's are pre-theoretical terms.

Thus, the basic principles of a theory cannot be conceived as an uninterpreted calculus, whose formulas contain, apart from logical or mathematical expressions, only theoretical

---

4. N. R. Campbell, whose construal of a scientific theory as consisting of a "hypothesis" and a "dictionary" is an early instance of a conception akin to that of Schema I, gives examples of just this type for the "hypotheses", i.e. calculi, of physical theories; see his *Foundations of Science* (formerly: *Physics, The Elements*); New York: Dover Publications, 1957, pp. 122–129.

terms which, formally, play the role of variables, and which obtain empirical relevance by way of correspondence principles.

It might be objected, in a spirit akin to that of operationism, that in this new context, the "old" terms p_1, p_2, $\ldots$, p_m represent new concepts, quite different from those they signify in their pre-theoretical employment. For the use of such terms as 'mass', 'velocity', 'energy', etc., in reference to atoms or subatomic particles requires entirely new operational criteria of application, since at the atomic and subatomic levels, the quantities in question cannot be measured by means of scales, electrometers, and the like, which afford operational criteria for their measurement at the pre-theoretical level. On the strict operationist maxim that different criteria of application determine different concepts, we would therefore have to conclude that, when used in internal principles, the terms p_1, p_2, $\ldots$, p_m stand for new concepts, quite different from those they signify in their pre-theoretical use. And we would have to add that it is therefore improper to use the old pre-theoretical terms in theoretical contexts: they should be replaced here by appropriate new terms, which, along with t_1, t_2, $\ldots$, t_k, would then belong to the theoretical vocabulary.

This does not seem to me a compelling argument, however. For, first of all, the operationist conception on which it is based is itself untenable. Suppose we tried to adhere strictly to the maxim that different operational criteria of application determine different concepts which, in principle, should be distinguished by the use of different terms such as 'tactual length' and 'optical length' in one of Bridgman's examples; [5] we would then be led to an infinite proliferation of concepts and corresponding terms, which would totally defeat the scien-

---

5. P. W. Bridgman, *The Logic of Modern Physics;* New York: The Macmillan Co., 1948; p. 16.

tific effort to find conceptually simple and economical theories that account for a great variety of empirical phenomena. For we would be obliged to say that the measurement of length, not only by means of rigid rods and by optical means, but even by rigid rods of different chemical composition or mass or date of manufacture, determines so many different concepts of length; and that weighing by means of two balances of however "identical" construction similarly determines different concepts of weight; for the two balances will always differ in some aspects, and will thus give rise to two different weighing operations. Hence, the operationist maxim we have considered is self-defeating. And in science any term is regarded, of course, as allowing for many alternative criteria of application. Each of these criteria is based on laws that connect the characteristic the term stands for (e.g., temperature) with observable phenomena of a certain kind (e.g., the readings of a mercury thermometer, a gas thermometer, a thermoelectric measuring device, etc.), which thus become indicators of the characteristic in question.

Moreover, the criteria of application are only part of the rules which govern the use of scientific terms, and which thus have a bearing on their "meanings": to a large extent, the use of a set of terms is determined by the general principles in which they function. Concerning the pre-theoretical and the theoretical uses of the terms $p_1, p_2, \ldots, p_m$, it seems therefore interesting and important to note that some of the basic theoretical laws that are applied to the concepts of mass, volume, velocity, energy, etc., in their internal, theoretical use are taken over from their pre-theoretical use. For example, in the classical kinetic theory, mass is taken to be additive in the sense that the mass of several molecules taken together is assumed to equal the sum of the masses of the individual molecules, just as the mass of a system consisting of several macroscopic physical bodies is taken to equal the sum of the masses of those bodies.[6] In fact, as a rule, this is not even explicitly stated: unless mention to the contrary is made, the attribution of mass to atoms and molecules is tacitly understood to imply the applicability of such fundamental laws in the new domain. Similarly, the conservation principles for mass, energy, and momentum are—at least initially—assumed to hold also for the atomic and molecular constituents of a gas, and so are the laws of motion.

In fact, the additivity principle for masses is used in three roles: initially as a pre-theoretical law governing the concept of mass; then, in the context of the kinetic theory, as an internal principle, as has just been noted; and finally, as a bridge principle. In this last role it implies, for example, that the mass of a body of gas equals the sum of the masses of its constituent molecules; it thus connects certain features of the theoretical scenario with corresponding features of macroscopic systems that can be described in pre-theoretical terms. This micro-macro applicability of the additivity principle is clearly presupposed in the explanation of the laws of multiple proportions and similarly in certain methods of determining Avogadro's number. These considerations strongly suggest that the term 'mass' (and others) can hardly be taken to stand for quite different concepts, depending on the kind of entity to which it is applied.

The transfer of basic pre-theoretical laws to the domain of the theoretical scenario is reminiscent of a principle normally observed when mathematical concepts are extended to a wider range of application; namely, the maxim that for the wider range, the concepts are to be construed in such a way as to

6. This additivity is not the same thing as the conservation of mass: even if the total mass of an isolated system consisting of several physical bodies always equals the sum of the masses of the components, the total mass might conceivably decrease in the course of time, and thus not be conserved, as a result, say, of the spontaneous disappearance of some of the components of the system.

ensure, as far as possible, the continued validity of the basic laws that govern them in their original area of application.

Thus, the notion of exponentiation for real numbers as arguments might first be introduced for the case where the exponents are natural numbers, a^m being defined, in effect, as a product of m factors, all of which equal a. For the operation thus specified, certain basic laws can then be proved, such as the following:

$$(1) \qquad \text{If } m > n, \text{ then } \frac{a^m}{a^n} = a^{m-n} \ (\text{for } a \neq 0)$$

(2)   If m is an integral multiple of n, then

$$\sqrt[n]{a^m} = a^{\frac{m}{n}}$$

When the question arises of extending the notion of exponentiation to a wider class of exponents—including 0, the negative integers, and all rational numbers, for example—the requisite definitions are chosen in such a way that the basic laws of exponentiation continue to hold in the new domain. Application of this requirement to (1) yields the following two formulas, which immediately provide the explicit definitions for a^0 and a^{-m}:

$$(3) \qquad a^0 = a^{m-m} = \frac{a^m}{a^m} = 1 \ \ (\text{for } a \neq 0)$$

$$(4) \quad a^{-m} = a^{0-m} = \frac{a^0}{a^m} = \frac{1}{a^m} \ \ (\text{for } a \neq 0)$$

Similarly, in consideration of (2) and (3), the principle requires that, for any two positive integers m and n, we set

$$(5) \qquad\qquad a^{\frac{m}{n}} = \sqrt[n]{a^m}$$

$$(6) \qquad\qquad a^{-\frac{m}{n}} = \frac{1}{\sqrt[n]{a^m}} \ (\text{for } a \neq 0)$$

There is a significant analogy between this way of extending mathematical concepts from a narrower to a wider domain of application and the manner in which the use of terms such as 'mass', 'momentum', and 'kinetic energy' is extended to a domain that includes atoms and molecules: in both cases, certain basic laws which hold in the original domain are carried over to the extended domain. And this preservation of laws surely affords grounds for saying that when the terms in question are applied in the new domain, they do not stand for entirely new and different concepts.

In our mathematical illustration, the narrower and the wider concepts of exponentiation are closely related; the former may, in fact, be considered a sub-concept of the latter. But the two are not identical: the "new" concept is applicable to a wider class of arguments, and some of the general principles that hold for the original concept (e.g., that a^m is a single-valued function of its two arguments) fail for the "new" one (in the class of real numbers, $a^{\frac{1}{2}}$ has two, one, or no values according as a is positive, zero, or negative).

In regard to the concepts of mass, velocity, etc., as used in the classical kinetic theory, however, a strong case could be made for holding that they are simply the same as those applied, in classical mechanics, to medium-sized objects. Classical mechanics imposes no lower bounds on the size or the mass of the bodies to which the concepts of mass, velocity, and kinetic energy can be significantly applied (in fact, Newtonian mechanics makes use of the concept of point masses); and the laws governing these concepts are subject to no such restrictions, either. This latter fact, incidentally, yields also a more direct retort to the operationist claim that the concept of mass as applied to atoms must be different from that applied to macroscopic bodies since the two cases require different operations of measurement: the application of classical mechanical considerations to the case of objects of the size of atoms shows that macroscopic scales are not sufficiently sensitive for weighing them, but that certain indirect procedures will provide an operational basis for determining their masses. It seems reasonable, therefore, to say that the need for different methods of determining masses does not indicate a difference in the meaning of 'mass' in the two cases, but only a large difference in the masses of the objects concerned. Of the classical kinetic theory of gases, then, it may be said that its internal principles characterize its theoretical scenario to a large extent with the help of the same concepts of mass, velocity, momentum, energy, and so forth that were already available at the pre-theoretical level. *A fortiori,* the internal principles do not just contain new theoretical terms, and it seems misleading, therefore, to view them, as is done in Schema I, as a system *C* of sentences containing only uninterpreted terms.

It is not so clear, however, whether an analogous argument applies in all other cases. More recent theories of the microstructure of matter, for example, acknowledge that the mass of any atomic nucleus is somewhat less than the sum of its constituent protons and neutrons taken separately; thus, these theories abandon the principle of additivity for the concept of mass, and they replace the principle of conservation of mass by the principle of conservation of mass-energy. Are we to say, then, that the term 'mass' as used in these theories has a different meaning—stands for a different concept—than the same word in its earlier scientific use (which is pre-theoretical in relation to these theories)? Or are we to say that the basic meaning of 'mass' has remained the same, and what has been changed is simply a set of—admittedly very far-reaching and fundamental—empirical assumptions about the one concept of mass to which the different theories refer?

The issue illustrated by this question has been widely discussed in recent years, and both of the positions just suggested have had their proponents. Hanson and Feyerabend, among others, have eloquently urged that the meanings of scientific terms depend on, and change with, the theories in which they function, and that even the meanings of so-called observational terms, which serve to describe the empirical evidence for or against a theory, are informed by the theory and change with it.[7] Feyerabend holds, for example, that temperature as conceived by Galileo and as supposedly measured by his thermoscope, is quite different from the current concept of temperature, since the theory of the relevant measurements has undergone considerable change; moreover, Feyerabend reasons that even the concept of temperature as used in classical thermodynamics is not the same as the one based on the kinetic theory of heat since, for example, the second law of thermodynamics holds as a strict universal law for the former, but not for the latter.[8]

Putnam, on the other hand, holds that the Italian word for 'temperature' as used by Galileo and the word 'temperature' as used today have the same "meaning", since they refer to the same physical magnitude, namely, "the magnitude whose greater and lower intensities are measured by the human sensorium as *warmer* and *colder* respectively." [9]

Now, it does seem to me suggestive and plausible to say that, in a somewhat elusive sense, Galileo's thermoscopic studies and more recent physical research on temperature are con-

7. See, for example, P. K. Feyerabend, "Explanation, Reduction, and Empiricism", in H. Feigl and G. Maxwell (eds.), *Minnesota Studies in the Philosophy of Science*, vol. III (Minneapolis: University of Minnesota Press, 1962), pp. 28–97; P. K. Feyerabend, "Reply to Criticism", in R. S. Cohen and M. W. Wartofsky (eds.), *Boston Studies in the Philosophy of Science*, Vol. II (New York: Humanities Press, 1965), pp. 223–261; N. R. Hanson, *Patterns of Discovery* (Cambridge, England: Cambridge University Press, 1958). For illuminating comments on the debate, and for further bibliographic references, see P. Achinstein, *op. cit.*, P. Achinstein, "On the Meaning of Scientific Terms", *The Journal of Philosophy* 61, 497–510 (1964), and D. Shapere, "Meaning and Scientific Change", in R. G. Colodny (ed.), *Mind and Cosmos;* (Pittsburgh: The University of Pittsburgh Press, 1966), pp. 41–85.
8. Cf. Feyerabend, *op. cit.*, (1962), p. 37 and pp. 78–84; also Section VI of Feyerabend, "Problems of Empiricism", in R. G. Colodny (ed.), *Beyond the Edge of Certainty;* Englewood Cliffs, N.J.: Prentice-Hall, 1965, pp. 145–260.
9. H. Putnam, "How Not to Talk about Meaning", in R. S. Cohen and M. W. Wartofsky (eds.), *Boston Studies in the Philosophy of Science*, vol. II. (New York: Humanities Press, 1965), pp. 205–222. Quoted passage, including italics, from p. 218.

cerned with the same quantitative characteristic of physical bodies; but I doubt that this statement admits of a very precise explication and defense. The argument offered by Putnam, for example, raises the question whether we are entitled to speak of "the" magnitude whose intensities are recorded by the human sensorium as warmer and colder: for this phrasing presupposes that there is one and only one such physical magnitude. But the intensity of the heat or cold we feel on touching a given object depends not only on its temperature, but also on its specific heat; it makes a great deal of difference whether our skin is in contact with air of $170°$ F or with water of the same temperature.

A clear analytic resolution of the issue would require an adequate explication of the notion of sameness of concepts or of the corresponding notion of the synonymy of terms; and it seems to me that no satisfactory general explications of these notions are currently available.

But no matter what position one may take concerning the extent to which pre-theoretical terms change their meanings when they are taken over by a theory, the considerations offered in this section show, I think, that it is misleading to view the internal principles of a theory as an uninterpreted calculus and the theoretical terms accordingly as variables, as markers of empty shells into which the juice of empirical content is pumped through the pipelines called correspondence rules.

5. NAGEL'S NOTION OF A MODEL AS A COMPONENT OF A THEORY.

Ernest Nagel, in his penetrating and carefully documented study of the structure of scientific theories, distinguishes three major components of a theory, namely (1) an abstract calculus that "implicitly defines" the basic notions of the system; (2) a set of "rules of correspondence", which assign an empirical content to the calculus by relating it to specific observational or experimental materials, and (3) a "model", which interprets the abstract calculus in terms of more or less familiar conceptual or visualizable materials.[10] In the case of the Bohr theory of the hydrogen atom, for example, the calculus would consist in the mathematical formulas constituting the basic equations of the theory; these will contain certain uninterpreted variables like 'r_i', 'E_j', 'λ'. The model specifies the conception, referred to earlier, of a hydrogen atom as consisting of a nucleus circled by an electron to which a series of discrete circular orbits are available, etc.; in this model, the variable 'r_i' is interpreted as the length of the radius of the ith orbit, 'E_j' as the total energy of the atom when the electron is in the jth orbit, 'λ' as the wave length of the radiation generated by an orbital jump, and so forth. The correspondence rules, finally, link the notion of specific orbital jumps of an electron to the experimental notion of corresponding particular spectral lines, and they establish other linkages of this kind.

The term 'model of a theory' has been used in a number of different senses. In one of its uses, it refers to such constructions as the mechanical models of electric currents or of the luminiferous ether that played a considerable role in the physics of the late 19th and early 20th centuries. Models of this kind carry an implicit 'as if' clause with them; thus, electric currents in wires behave in certain respects as if they consisted in the flow of a liquid through pipes of various widths and under various pressures, etc. But these models clearly were not intended to represent the actual micro-structure of the modelled phenomena: wires were not thought actually to be pipes, and the ether was not believed actually to consist of the components envisaged by one model, namely, sets of nested hollow spheres, separated by elastic springs. The kinetic theory of gases, on the other hand,—and, I think, similarly Bohr's

---

10. See E. Nagel, *op. cit.,* especially chapter 5.

model of atomic structure—does put forward a conjecture as to the actual microstructure of the objects under study: gases are claimed actually to consist of molecules moving about, and colliding, at various high speeds; atoms are claimed actually to have certain specific subatomic constituents and to be capable of certain discrete energy states.[11] To be sure, these claims, like those of any other empirical hypothesis, may subsequently be amplified and refined or modified or partly discarded (as happened to Bohr's model), but they form an integral part of the theory. Models of the former kind, on the other hand, consist in physical systems which exhibit certain material analogies to the phenomena under study or whose behavior is governed by laws having the same mathematical form as basic laws of the theory. Such models may be of considerable psychological interest and heuristic value; they may make it easier to grasp a new theory and to become familiar with it, and they may suggest various consequences and even extensions of the basic assumptions of the theory; but they are not part of the content of the theory and are, thus, logically dispensable.[12]

For this reason I will restrict the following remarks to those cases where the "model" expresses part of the content of the theory, as in the kinetic theory of gases, the classical wave and particle theories of light, the molecular-lattice theory of crystal structure, recent theories of the molecular structure of genes and the basis of the genetic code, and I take it, in Bohr's theory of atomic structure.

In regard to the latter, Nagel notes that, usually, the theory is not presented as an abstract set of postulates supplemented by rules of correspondence, but is embedded in the model

11. This idea is lucidly developed, in the context of a distinction of four senses of 'model of a theory', in M. Spector, "Models and Theories", *The British Journal for the Philosophy of Science* 16, 121–142 (1965).
12. For fuller discussions of these issues, see, for example, E. Nagel, *op. cit.,* pp. 107–117; M. B. Hesse, *Models and Analogies in Science;* London and New York: Sheed and Ward, 1963; C. G. Hempel, *Aspects of Scientific Explanation;* New York: The Free Press, 1965, pp. 433–447.

mentioned above because, among other reasons, it can thus be understood with greater ease than can the inevitably more complex formal exposition.[13] But for the reasons outlined earlier, I think their significance goes further. By characterizing certain theoretical variables as masses, energies, and the like, the theory commits itself to extending to these variables certain laws characteristic of those concepts or, if some of these laws are suspended, to making the appropriate modifications explicit (as happens in Bohr's model, where, in contrast to the principles of classical electromagnetic theory, an orbiting electron is assumed not to radiate energy). Thus, the specification of the model determines in part what consequences can be inferred from the theory and hence, what the theory can explain or predict.

I will try to state the point at issue in yet another way. The postulates of the formal calculus of a theory are often said to constitute implicit definitions of its basic terms: they rule out all those conceivable interpretations of the primitive terms which would turn some of the postulates into false statements.

Thus, the single postulate that an—otherwise unspecified —relation R is asymmetrical limits the possible interpretations of 'R' and thereby "implicity defines" it or partially specifies its meaning; for example, the postulate precludes the interpretation, by model or by correspondence rules, of 'Rxy' as 'x resembles y', 'x respects y', 'x is adjacent to y', and so forth. But the model of a theory in the sense here at issue imposes similar constraints on the empirical content that may be assigned to theoretical terms by means of correspondence rules. Thus, the "interpretation", by the "model", of certain theoretical magnitudes as masses and charges of particles precludes the adoption of correspondence rules that would assign to those magnitudes the physical dimensions of mass densities and temperatures. Moreover, the masses and charges of par-

---

13. E. Nagel, *op. cit.,* p. 95.

ticles would have to be linked by suitable composition laws to macroscopically ascertainable masses and charges; and so forth. Thus, the statements of such a model are not only of heuristic value: they have a systematic-logical function much like the formulas of the calculus. And this seems to me to remove one further reason against conceiving what I called the internal principles of a theory as divided into a calculus and a model.

6. THE STATUS OF BRIDGE PRINCIPLES.

In Schema I, the sentences in *R* are regarded as statements that assign empirical content to the terms of the calculus; and the use of such designations for them as 'operational *definition*', 'coordinating *definition*', '*rule* of correspondence' tends to convey the suggestion that they have the character of stipulations or, more accurately, of statements made true by definition or by terminological conventions of a more general kind; a similar impression is created by Campbell's construal of them as a "dictionary" that serves to relate the "hypothesis" of a theory to (pre-theoretical) empirical propositions. This construal is definitely not intended or endorsed by all proponents of the idea of correspondence rules; and it is surely untenable for several reasons, among them the following:

As was said earlier, the basic principles of a theory often assert the existence of certain kinds of entities and processes, which are characterized, to a greater or lesser extent, by means of antecedently understood empirical concepts; and the so-called coordinating principles then have the character of hypotheses expressing specific connections between the entities and processes posited by the theory and certain phenomena that have been examined "pre-theoretically". But not all these connecting hypotheses can have the non-empirical status of truths by terminological convention. For quite often, a theory

provides us with several principles that link a theoretical notion
to different potential observational or experimental findings.
For example, physical theory offers several different ways of
determining Avogadro's number or the charge of an electron
or the velocity of light; this implies the claim that if one of
the experimental methods yields a certain numerical value for
the magnitude in question, then the alternative methods will
yield the same value: but whether this is in fact the case surely
is an empirical matter and cannot be settled by definitions,
rules, or stipulations. It was precisely in order to avoid the
intrusion of this empirical element, and the associated inductive "risk", that Bridgman regarded different operational procedures as specifying different concepts. On the other hand,
when Carnap, in "Testability and Meaning", offered the basis
for a logically much more subtle and supple restatement of the
idea of an operational specification of meaning, he noted explicitly that when a term is introduced by means of several
reduction sentences (the counterparts, in his theory, of operational definitions), then the latter usually have empirical consequences, expressible by a well-defined sentence which he
calls the representative sentence of that set of reduction
sentences.[14]

Still another consideration is relevant here. Even if a "rule
of correspondence" is initially established by stipulative *fiat,* it
may lose its status as true by convention, and become liable
to modification in response to empirical evidence or theoretical developments. For example, to mark off, or "define" in
experimental terms, equal intervals of time, some periodic
process must be chosen to serve as a standard clock, such as
the daily apparent motion of a star, or the swinging of a pendulum. The time intervals determined by the recurring phases of

14. See R. Carnap, "Testability and Meaning", *Philosophy of Science,* 3, 419–471
(1936) and 4, 1–40 (1937); especially p. 451. Carnap has since then developed his
analysis of this topic further; for a recent statement, see section 24 (pp. 958–966)
of his "Replies and Systematic Expositions" in P. A. Schilpp (ed.) *The Philosophy
of Rudolf Carnap* (La Salle, Illinois; Open Court, 1963).

the chosen process are then equal by convention or stipulation. But what particular standard clock (and rule of correspondence specifying it) is chosen may make a great deal of difference for the possibility of formulating a system of simple and comprehensive laws and theoretical principles concerning the time dependence of empirical phenomena. For example, if the pulse beat of a particular person were chosen as the standard, then the "speed", the temporal rate of change, of all empirical phenomena would become causally linked to the state of health of the person chosen as the standard clock, and it would be impossible to formulate any simple laws of free fall, of planetary motion, of harmonic oscillation, of radioactive decay, etc. But even a perfectly plausible choice of standard clocks, such as the rotating earth or a pendulum device, leads to basically similar consequences: The rate of the earth's rotation is known to be slowly decreasing, and the period of a pendulum is dependent on several extraneous factors, such as location (since the gravitational force acting on the pendulum bob varies with the location). The theoretical principles and the empirical considerations that indicate these deviations and determine them quantitatively may well have grown out of findings obtained with the help of clocks of the incriminated kind; but theoretical consistency demands that those clocks, and hence the associated correspondence rules, now be qualified as only approximately correct, and that new, more accurate, methods of measurement be specified.

Thus, even though a sentence may originally be introduced by stipulation, and may thus reflect a rule of correspondence in the narrower sense of 'rule', it soon joins the club of all other member-statements of the theory and becomes subject to revision in response to further empirical findings and theoretical developments; and the bridge principles of Schema II are conceived as having this character.

It might seem that the preceding argument about the change of status of statements first established by stipulation, is flawed by confounding logical and epistemological questions with genetic-pragmatic ones. But the point can be argued without offering grounds for this suspicion: Even if we imagine a scientific theory "frozen", if we consider its form and status at one particular stage, there are no clear ways of distinguishing those statements of the theory which are made true by rule or convention from those which are not. The initially plausible idea that statements of the first kind should not be liable to modification in response to empirical evidence, will not serve the purpose, as we have noted: no statements other than the truths of logic and mathematics come with such a guarantee.

The considerations presented in support of Schema II have still another consequence; they show that within the class T of statements that constitute a theory, the dividing line between the two subclasses I and B is not very sharply determined. In particular, it cannot be characterized syntactically, by reference to the constituent terms; for, as we noted, sentences in either class contain theoretical terms characteristic of the theory as well as pre-theoretical terms. Nor is the difference one of epistemic status, such as stipulational *vs.* empirical truth.

The distinction between the internal principles and the bridge principles of a theory must be understood in the somewhat intuitive manner in which it was introduced earlier in this essay. It is thus a vague distinction, but to the extent that the preceding considerations are sound, it can none the less provide philosophic illumination.

W. V. Quine

STIMULUS

AND

MEANING*

EPISTEMOLOGY, or the theory of knowledge, is concerned with the foundations of science. Conceived thus broadly, epistemology includes the study of the foundations of mathematics as one of its departments. Specialists at the turn of the century thought that their efforts in this particular department were achieving notable success: mathematics seemed to reduce altogether to logic. In a more recent perspective this reduction is seen to be better describable as a reduction to logic and set theory. This correction is a disappointment epistemologically, since the firmness and obviousness that we associate with logic cannot be claimed for set theory. But still the success achieved in the foundations of mathematics remains exemplary by comparative standards, and we can illuminate the rest of epistemology somewhat by drawing parallels to this department.

Studies in the foundations of mathematics divide sym-

*A revised version of the first five sixths of this lecture has meanwhile been presented along with some added material as an address under the title "Epistemology Naturalized" and published in the Proceedings of the XIVth International Congress of Philosophy, Vienna, 1968.

metrically into two sorts: conceptual and doctrinal. The conceptual studies are concerned with meaning, the doctrinal with truth. The conceptual studies are concerned with clarifying concepts by defining them, some in terms of others. The doctrinal studies are concerned with establishing laws by proving them, some on the basis of others. Ideally the obscurer concepts would be defined in terms of the clearer ones so as to maximize clarity, and the less obvious laws would be proved from the more obvious ones so as to maximize certainty. Ideally the definitions would generate all the concepts from clear and distinct ideas, and the proofs would generate all the theorems from self-evident axioms.

The two ideals are linked. For, if you define all the concepts by use of some favored subset of them, you thereby show how to translate all theorems into these favored terms. The clearer these terms are, the likelier it is that the truths couched in them will be obviously true, or derivable from obvious truths. If in particular the concepts of mathematics were all reducible to the clear terms of logic, then all the truths of mathematics would go over into truths of logic; and surely the truths of logic are all obvious or at least potentially obvious, i.e., derivable from obvious truths by individually obvious steps.

This particular outcome is in fact denied us, of course, since mathematics reduces only to set theory and not to logic proper. Such reduction still enhances clarity, but only because of the interrelations that emerge and not because the end terms of the analysis are clearer than others. As for the end truths, the axioms of set theory, these have less obviousness and certainty to recommend them than do most of the mathematical theorems that we would derive from them. Moreover, we know from Gödel's work that no consistent axiom system can cover mathematics even when we renounce self-evidence. Reduction in the foundations of mathematics remains mathematically and philosophically fascinating, but it does not do what the epistemologist would like of it: it does not reveal the ground of mathematical knowledge, it does not show how mathematical certainty is possible.

Still there remains a helpful thought, regarding epistemology generally, in that duality of structure which was especially conspicuous in the foundations of mathematics. I refer to the bifurcation into a theory of concepts, or meaning, and a theory of doctrine, or truth; for this applies to the epistemology of natural knowledge no less than to the foundations of mathematics. The epistemologists of natural knowledge want to base our knowledge of nature on sense experience. This means explaining the notion of body and related notions in sensory terms; this is the conceptual side. And then, on the doctrinal side, there is the problem of justifying in sensory terms our knowledge of truths about nature.

On the conceptual side, Hume's method of reduction was bold and simple: he identified the material objects outright with the sense impressions. If common sense distinguishes between the material apple and our sense impressions of it on the ground that the apple is one and enduring while the impressions are many and fleeting, then, Hume held, so much the worse for common sense; the notion of its being the same apple on one occasion and another is a vulgar confusion.

Nearly a century after Hume's *Treatise,* the same view of bodies was espoused by the early American philosopher Alexander Bryan Johnson. "The word iron names an associated sight and feel," Johnson wrote.

What then of the doctrinal side, the justification of our knowledge of truths about nature? Here Hume despaired. By his identification of bodies with impressions he did succeed in construing some singular statements about bodies as indubitable truths, yes; as truths about impressions, directly known. But general statements, also singular statements about the future, gained no increment of certainty by being construed as about impressions; for Hume saw no rational basis for predicting what impressions might come.

On the doctrinal side, I do not see that we are farther

along today than where Hume left us. The Humean predicament is the human predicament. But on the conceptual side
there has been progress. There the crucial step forward was
made already before Alexander Bryan Johnson's day, although Johnson did not emulate it. It was made by Bentham
in his theory of fictions. Bentham's step was the recognition
of contextual definition, or what he called *paraphrasis*. He
recognized that to explain a term we do not need to specify an
object for it to refer to, nor even specify a synonymous word
or phrase; we need only show, by whatever means, how to
translate all the whole sentences in which the term is to be
used. Hume's and Johnson's desperate measure of identifying
bodies with impressions ceased to be the only conceivable way
of making sense of talk of bodies, even granted that impressions were the only reality. One could undertake to explain
talk of bodies in terms of talk of impressions by translating
one's whole sentences about bodies into whole sentences about
impressions, without equating the bodies themselves to anything at all.

   This idea of contextual definition, or recognition of the
sentence as the primary vehicle of meaning, was indispensable
to the ensuing developments in the foundations of mathematics. It was explicit in Frege, and it attained its full flower
in Russell's doctrine of singular descriptions as incomplete
symbols.

   Contextual definition was one of two resorts that could be
expected to have a liberating effect upon the conceptual side
of the epistemology of natural knowledge. The other is resort
to the resources of set theory as auxiliary concepts. The epistemologist who is willing to eke out his austere ontology of
sense impressions with these set-theoretic auxiliaries is suddenly rich: he has not just his impressions to play with, but
sets of them, and sets of sets, and so on up. Constructions in
the foundations of mathematics have shown that such set-
theoretic aids are a powerful addition; after all, the entire

glossary of concepts of classical mathematics is constructible from them. Thus equipped, our epistemologist may not need either to identify bodies with impressions or to settle for contextual definition; he may hope to find in some subtle construction of sets upon sets upon sets of sense impressions a category of objects enjoying just the formal properties that he wants for bodies.

The two resorts are very unequal in epistemological status. Contextual definition is unassailable. Sentences that have been given meaning as wholes are undeniably meaningful, and the use they make of their component terms is therefore meaningful, regardless of whether any translations are offered for those terms in isolation. Surely Hume and A. B. Johnson would have used contextual definition with pleasure if they had thought of it. Recourse to sets, on the other hand, is a drastic ontological move, a retreat from the austere ontology of impressions. There are philosophers who would rather settle for bodies outright than accept all these sets, which amount, after all, to the whole abstract ontology of mathematics.

This issue has not always been clear, however, owing to deceptive hints of continuity between elementary logic and set theory. This is why mathematics was once believed to reduce to logic, that is, to an innocent and unquestionable logic, and to inherit these qualities. And this is probably why Russell was content to resort to sets as well as to contextual definition when in *Our Knowledge of the External World* and elsewhere he addressed himself to the epistemology of natural knowledge, on its conceptual side.

To account for the external world as a logical construct of sense data—such, in Russell's terms, was the program. It was Carnap, in his *Der logische Aufbau der Welt* of 1928, who came nearest to executing it.

This was the conceptual side of epistemology; what of the doctrinal? There the Humean predicament remained unaltered. Carnap's constructions, if carried successfully to completion, would have enabled us to translate all sentences about the world into terms of sense data, or observation, plus logic and set theory. But the mere fact that a sentence is *couched* in terms of observation, logic, and set theory does not mean that it can be *proved* from observation sentences by logic and set theory. The most modest of generalizations about observable traits will cover more cases than its utterer can have had occasion actually to observe. By Carnap's day the hopelessness of grounding natural science upon immediate experience in a firmly logical way was acknowledged. The Cartesian quest for certainty had been the remote motivation of epistemology, both on its conceptual and its doctrinal side; but by now that quest was seen as a lost cause. To endow the truths of nature with the full authority of immediate experience was as forlorn a hope as hoping to endow the truths of mathematics with the potential obviousness of elementary logic.

What then could motivate Carnap's heroic efforts on the conceptual side of epistemology, when hope of certainty on the doctrinal side was abandoned? There were two good reasons still. One was that such constructions could be expected to elicit and clarify the sensory evidence for science, even if the inferential steps between sensory evidence and scientific doctrine must fall short of certainty. The other reason was that such constructions would deepen our understanding of our discourse about the world, even apart from questions of evidence; it would make all cognitive discourse as clear as observation terms and logic, and, I must regretfully add, set theory.

It was a gloomy day in the annals of epistemology when we had to acquiesce in the impossibility of strictly deriving the science of the external world from sensory evidence. Two cardinal tenets of empiricism remained unassailable, however, and so remain to this day. One is that whatever evidence there *is* for science *is* sensory evidence. The other, to which I shall recur, is that all inculcation of meanings of words must rest ultimately on sensory evidence. Hence the continuing attractiveness of the idea of a *logischer Aufbau* in which the sensory content of discourse would stand forth explicitly.

If Carnap had successfully carried such a construction through, how could he have told whether it was the right one? The question would have had no point. He was seeking what he called a *rational reconstruction*. Any construction of physicalistic discourse in terms of sense experience, logic, and set theory would have been seen as satisfactory if it made the physicalistic discourse come out right. If there is one way there are many, but any would be a great achievement.

But why all this creative reconstruction, all this make-believe? The stimulation of his sensory receptors is all anybody has had to go on, ultimately, in arriving at his picture of the world. Why not just see how this construction really proceeds? Why not settle for psychology? Such a surrender of the epistemological burden to psychology is a move that was denounced by Lotze, Frege, and others in the nineteenth century under the disparaging name of psychologism, partly for fear of circular reasoning. If the epistemologist's goal is validation of the grounds of empirical science, he defeats his purpose by using psychology or other empirical science in the validation. However, such scruples against circularity have little point once we have stopped dreaming of deducing science from observations. If we are out simply to understand the link between observation and science, we are well advised to use any available information, including that provided by the very science whose link with observation we are seeking to understand. We should favor psychologism.

But there remains a different reason, unconnected with fears of circularity or of psychologism, for still favoring creative reconstruction. We should like to be able to *translate* science into logic and observation terms and set theory. This would be a great epistemological achievement, for it would show all the rest of the concepts of science to be theoretically superfluous. It would legitimize them—to whatever degree the concepts of set theory, logic, and observation are themselves legitimate—by showing that everything done with the one apparatus could in principle be done with the other. If psychology itself could deliver a truly translational reduction of this kind, we should welcome it; but certainly it cannot, for certainly we did not grow up learning definitions of physicalistic language in terms of a prior language of set theory, logic, and observation. Here, then, would be a good reason for persisting in a rational reconstruction: we want to establish the essential innocence of physical concepts, by showing them to be theoretically dispensable.

The fact is, though, that the construction which Carnap outlined in *Der logische Aufbau der Welt* does not give translational reduction either. It would not even if the outline were filled in. The crucial point comes where Carnap is explaining how to assign sense qualities to positions in physical space and time. These assignments are to be made in such a way as to fulfill, as well as possible, certain desiderata which he states, and with growth of experience the assignments are to be revised to suit. This plan, however illuminating, does not offer any key to *translating* the sentences of science into terms of observation, logic, and set theory.

We must despair of any such reduction. Carnap had despaired of it by 1936, when, in "Testability and Meaning," he introduced so-called *reduction forms* of a type weaker than definition. Definitions had shown always how to translate sentences into equivalent sentences. Contextual definition of a term showed how to translate sentences containing the term into equivalent sentences lacking the term. Reduction forms of Carnap's liberalized kind, on the other hand, do not in general give equivalences; they give implications. They explain a new term, if only partially, by specifying some sentences which are implied by sentences containing the term, and other sentences which imply sentences containing the term.

It is tempting to suppose that the countenancing of reduction forms in this liberal sense is just one further step of liberalization comparable to the earlier one, taken by Bentham, of countenancing contextual definition. The former and sterner kind of rational reconstruction might have been represented as a fictitious history in which we imagined our ancestors introducing the terms of physicalistic discourse on a phenomenalistic and set-theoretic basis by a succession of contextual definitions. The new and more liberal kind of rational reconstruction is a fictitious history in which we imagine our ancestors introducing those terms by a succession rather of reduction forms of the weaker sort.

This, however, is a wrong comparison. The fact is rather that the former and sterner kind of rational reconstruction, where definition reigned, embodied no fictitious history at all. It was nothing more nor less than a set of directions—or would have been, if successful—for accomplishing everything in terms of phenomena and set theory that we now accomplish in terms of the external world. It would have been a true reduction by translation, a legitimation by elimination. *Definire est eliminare*. Rational reconstruction by Carnap's later and looser reduction forms does none of this.

To relax the demand for definition, and settle for a kind of reduction that does not eliminate, is to renounce the last remaining advantage that we supposed rational reconstruction to have over straight psychology; namely, the advantage of translational reduction. If all we hope for is a reconstruction that links science to experience in explicit ways short of translation, then it would seem more sensible to settle for psychology. Better to discover how science is in fact developed and learned than to fabricate a fictitious structure to a similar effect.

The empiricist made one major concession when he despaired of deducing the truths of nature from sensory evidence. In despairing now even of translating those truths into terms of observation and logico-mathematical auxiliaries, he makes another major concession. For suppose we hold, with the old empiricist Charles Sanders Peirce, that the very meaning of a statement consists in the difference its truth would make to possible experience. Might we not formulate, in a chapter-length sentence in observational language, all the difference that the truth of a given statement might make to experience, and might we not then take all this as the translation? Even if the difference that the truth of the statement would make to experience ramifies indefinitely, we might still hope to embrace it all in the logical implications of our chapter-length formulation, just as we can axiomatize an infinity of theorems. In giving up hope of such translation, then, the empiricist is conceding that the empirical meanings of typical statements about the external world are inaccessible and ineffable.

How is this inaccessibility to be explained? Simply on the ground that the experiential implications of a typical statement about bodies are too complex for finite axiomatization, however lengthy? No; I have a different explanation. It is that the typical statement about bodies has no fund of experiential implications it can call its own. A substantial mass of theory, taken together, will commonly have experiential implications; this is how we make verifiable predictions. We may not be able to explain why we arrive at theories which make success-ful predictions, but we do. Sometimes also an experience implied by a theory fails to come off; and then, ideally, we declare the theory false. But the failure falsifies only a block of theory as a whole, a conjunction of many statements. The failure shows that one or more of those statements is false, but it does not show which. The predicted experiences, true and false, are not implied by any one of the component statements of the theory rather than another. The component statements simply do not have empirical meanings, by Peirce's standard; but a sufficiently inclusive portion of theory does. If we can aspire to a sort of *logischer Aufbau der Welt* at all, it must be to one in which the texts slated for translation into observational and logico-mathematical terms are mostly broad theories taken as wholes, rather than just terms or short sentences. The translation of a theory would be a ponderous axiomatization of all the experiential difference that the truth of the theory would make. It would be a queer translation, for it would translate the whole but none of the parts. We might better speak in such a case not of translation but simply of observational evidence for theories; and we may, following Peirce, still fairly call this the empirical meaning of the theories.

These considerations raise a philosophical question even about ordinary unphilosophical translation, such as from English into Arunta or Chinese. For, if the English sentences of a theory have their meaning only together as a body, then we can justify their translation into Arunta only together as a body. There will be no justification for pairing off the component English sentences with component Arunta sentences, except as these correlations make the translation of the theory as a whole come out right. Any translations of the English sentences into Arunta sentences will be as correct as any other, so long as the net empirical implications of the theory as a whole are preserved in translation. But it is to be expected that many different ways of translating the component sentences, essentially different individually, would deliver the same empirical implications for the theory as a whole; deviations in the translation of one component sentence could be compensated for in the translation of another component sentence. Insofar, no ground remains for saying which of two glaringly unlike translations of individual sentences is right. Such is the doctrine which I have urged elsewhere under the title of the *indeterminacy of translation*.

This reasoning depends on an empirical theory of meaning. Should the unwelcomeness of the conclusion persuade us to abandon the empirical theory of meaning? Certainly not.

The sort of meaning that is basic to translation, and to the learning of one's own language, is necessarily empirical meaning and nothing more. A child learns his first words and sentences by hearing and using them in the presence of appropriate stimuli. These must be external stimuli, for they must act both on the child and on the speaker from whom he is learning. It is only thus that the child can associate the sentence with the same stimulus that elicited the sentence from the teacher, and it is only thus that the teacher can know whether to reinforce or discourage the child's utterances. In these transactions a speaker's subjective imagery is beside the point. Language is socially inculcated and controlled; the inculcation and control turn strictly on the keying of sentences to shared stimulation. Internal factors may vary *ad libitum* without prejudice to communication as long as the keying of language to external stimuli is undisturbed. Surely one has no choice but to be an empiricist so far as one's theory of linguistic meaning is concerned.

What I have said of infant learning applies equally to the linguist's learning of a new language in the field. If the linguist does not lean on related languages for which there are previously established translation practices, then obviously he has no data but the concomitances of native utterance and observable stimulus situation. No wonder there is indeterminacy of translation—for of course only a small fraction of our utterances report concurrent external stimulation. Granted, the linguist will end up with unequivocal translations of everything; but only by making many arbitrary choices—arbitrary even though unconscious—along the way. Arbitrary? By this I mean that essentially different choices could still have made everything come out right that is susceptible in principle of any kind of check.

Let me link up, in a different order, some of the points I have made. The crucial consideration behind my argument for the indeterminacy of translation was that a statement about the world does not always or usually have a separable fund of empirical consequences that it can call its own. That consideration served also to account for the impossibility of an epistemological reduction of the sort where every sentence is equated to a sentence in observational and logico-mathematical terms. And the impossibility of that sort of epistemological reduction dissipated the last advantage that rational reconstruction seemed to have over psychology; it conquered our last scruple against unbridled psychologism.

Philosophers have rightly despaired of translating everything into observational and logico-mathematical terms. They have despaired of this even when they have not recognized, as the reason for this irreducibility, that the statements largely do not have their private bundles of empirical consequences. And some philosophers have seen in this irreducibility the bankruptcy of epistemology. Carnap and the other logical positivists of the Vienna circle had already pressed the term 'metaphysics' into pejorative use, as connoting meaninglessness; and the term 'epistemology' was next. Wittgenstein and his followers, mainly at Oxford, found a residual philosophical vocation in therapy: in curing philosophers of the delusion that there were epistemological problems.

Epistemological nihilism flourishes also outside the spheres of influence of Oxford and Vienna. In books on scientific method by Michael Polanyi, Thomas Kuhn, and others there is a tendency to belittle the role of evidence and to accentuate cultural relativism. Norwood Russell Hanson ventures even to discredit the idea of observation itself. The difficulty adduced regarding observation is that so-called observations vary from observer to observer with the amount of knowledge that the observers bring with them. The veteran physicist looks at some apparatus and sees an x-ray tube. The neophyte, looking at the same place, observes rather "a glass and metal instrument replete with wires, reflectors, screws, lamps, and pushbuttons." One man's observation is another man's closed book or flight of fancy. The notion of observation, as the impartial and objective source of evidence for science, is bankrupt.

There is melancholy irony here. Finding the old epistemology untenable as a whole, philosophers react by repudiating parts which, if freed of the rest, could become clear and sound as never before.

The notion of observation is a case in point. Our retinas are irradiated in two dimensions, yet we see things as three-dimensional without conscious inference. Which is to count as observation—the unconscious two-dimensional reception or the conscious three-dimensional apprehension? In the old epistemological context the conscious form had priority; for we were out to justify our knowledge of the external world by rational construction, and that demands awareness. And if awareness is demanded, then Hanson's complaint is sustained.

What Hanson and company fail to take into account is that with the passing of the old epistemology there ceases to be any reason to count awareness an essential trait of observation. Awareness ceased to be demanded when we gave up trying to justify our knowledge of the external world by rational reconstruction. What is to count as observation now can be settled in terms of the stimulation of sensory receptors, let consciousness fall where it may. What was for old epistemologists a vicious circle—this appeal to physical stimulation in an account of our knowledge of the physical world—should be perfectly welcome now that we have stopped dreaming of deducing science from sense data. We are after an understanding of science as an institution or process in the world, and we do not intend that understanding to be any better than the science which is its object. Let us by all means equate our observations to stimulations of our sensory receptors, or talk of stimulations instead of observations, if it helps.

It helps. Unconscious inference can now be taken in

stride. The trained physicist and the layman get the same stimulations, nearly enough, and no problem is raised by the fact that the physicist says or thinks "x-ray" while the layman does not. The Gestalt psychologists' challenge to sensory atomism, which seemed so relevant to epistemology forty years ago, is likewise deactivated. Regardless of whether sensory atoms or Gestalten are what favor the forefront of our consciousness, it is simply the stimulations of our sensory receptors that are best looked upon as the input to our cognitive mechanism. Old paradoxes about unconscious data and inference, old problems about chains of inference that would have to be completed too quickly—these no longer matter.

In the old anti-psychologistic days the question of epistemological priority was moot. What is epistemologically prior to what? Are Gestalten prior to sensory atoms because they are noticed, or should we favor sensory atoms on some more subtle ground? Now that we are permitted to appeal to physical stimulation, the problem dissolves; A is epistemologically prior to B if A is causally nearer than B to the sensory receptors. Or, what is in some ways better, just talk explicitly in terms of causal proximity to sensory receptors and drop the talk of epistemological priority.

There are also other aids, besides talk of sensory receptors, which accrue to the theory of perception once we lift all restraints on physical reference. Here is a small illustration of another kind. All will agree that when we say we see a child in a picture we are really seeing only the picture, not the child. But there is some indecision over how to characterize the seeing of a child in a mirror: are we seeing a patch of mirror colored by the light from the child or are we seeing the child himself along a crooked line of sight? Even in this statement of the quandary there is physical reference, but it is restrained: the seen physical objects are set opposite the subject's sense data with a minimum of attention to the intervening physical laws and circumstances. If we attend more to these, the quandary resolves itself. The preferable version of the mirror phenomenon is that we see the child himself along the crooked line of sight; and the decisive consideration is focal length. You cannot scrutinize the image more closely by training a reading glass on the mirror; you can by training opera glasses on it. This consideration, while far from profound, takes the physical context more seriously than would have accorded with old epistemological patterns.

Around 1932 there was debate in the Vienna circle over what to count as observation sentences, or *Protokollsätze*. One position was that they had the form of reports of sense impressions. Another was that they were statements of an elementary sort about the external world, e.g., "A red cube is standing on the table." Another, Otto Neurath's, was that they had the form of reports of relations between percipients and external things: "Otto now sees a red cube on the table." The worst of it was that there seemed to be no objective way of settling the matter: no way of making real sense of the question.

Let us now try to view the matter unreservedly in the context of the external world. Vaguely speaking, what we want of observation sentences is that they be the ones in closest causal proximity to the sensory receptors. But how is such proximity to be gauged? The idea may be rephrased this way: observation sentences are sentences which, as we learn language, are most strongly conditioned to concurrent sensory stimulation rather than to stored collateral information. Thus let us imagine a sentence queried for our verdict as to whether it is true or false; queried for our assent or dissent. Then the sentence is an observation sentence if our verdict depends only on the sensory stimulation present at the time.

But a verdict cannot depend on present sensory stimulation to the exclusion of stored information. The very fact of our having learned the language evinces much storing of information, and of information without which we should be in no position to give verdicts on sentences however observational. So we must further shore up our definition of observation sentence. What characterizes observation sentences, ideally, is that our verdicts on those sentences depend on present sensory stimulation and on no collateral information except what goes into understanding the sentences. But how are we to distinguish between the information that merely goes into understanding a sentence and information that goes beyond?

This is the problem of distinguishing between analytic truth, which issues from the mere meanings of the component words, and synthetic truth, which depends on more than meanings. Now a criterion to somewhat this purpose is afforded by the social character of language. The analytic truths will tend, at least when simple, to be subscribed to by all fluent communicants of the speech community, while the synthetic ones will largely not be.

There is no denying that this criterion fits preconceptions poorly. Community-wide platitudes, such as that there are or have been black dogs, get counted as analytic. This is good reason to by-pass the term 'analytic.' By-passing terms cannot, indeed, conceal that we have drawn no line between what goes into the mere understanding of the sentences of a language and what else the community sees eye-to-eye on. But this lack of a boundary is a lack that I am inclined to condone. I doubt that an objective distinction can be made between meaning and such collateral information as is community-wide.

Turning back then to our task of defining observation sentences, we get this: an observation sentence is one on which all speakers of the language give the same verdict when given the same concurrent stimulation.

This formulation accords perfectly with the traditional role of the observation sentence as the court of appeal of scientific theories. For by our definition the observation sentences are the sentences on which all members of the community will agree under uniform stimulation. And note that there is generally no subjectivity in the phrasing of such sentences; they will usually be about bodies. After all, it is to discourse about bodies, and not about sense data, that we are first conditioned in our learning of language; for the inculcation of language is a social affair, and it is bodies that are out there for society to share. Since the distinguishing trait of an observation sentence is intersubjective agreement under agreeing stimulation, a corporeal subject matter is likelier than not.

The old tendency to associate observation sentences with a subjective sensory subject matter is rather an irony when we reflect that observation sentences are also meant to be the intersubjective tribunal of scientific hypotheses. The old tendency was due to the drive to base science on something firmer and prior in the subject's experience; but we dropped that project.

Does any place remain for the old epistemological ontology of sense data, or sensa? Seen from the point of view of our now acknowledged position amid the objects of the external world, a sense datum would be a state of an organ or organism. Sense data would be, in Skinner's phrase, intervening variables between stimulus and response. Now what goes on between stimulus and response, between input and output, is certainly a worthy question for investigation and hypothesis; and the physiologists and psychologists are on the job. In the best eventual theory of the matter the intervening variables may prove reminiscent somehow of the old epistemologists' sense data, and then again they may not.

Be that as it may, there is meanwhile much more to say of observation sentences. I regret that part of what follows will have to be a summary of technical matters in *Word and Object* which some of you already know.

Our acceptance of psychologism worked wonders in clarifying the notion of observation sentence. But is this good, is the notion useful? Yes, it is fundamental in two connections, and these two correspond to the duality that I remarked upon early in this lecture: the duality between concept and doctrine, between knowing what a sentence means and knowing whether it is true. The observation sentence is basic to both enterprises. Its relation to doctrine, to our knowledge of what is true, is very much the traditional one: observation sentences are the repository of evidence for scientific hypotheses.

Its relation to meaning is fundamental too, since observation sentences are the ones we are in a position to learn to understand first, both as children and as field linguists. For observation sentences are precisely the ones that we can correlate with observable circumstances of the occasion of utterance or assent, independently of variations in the past histories of individual informants. They afford the only entry to language.

The observation sentence is the cornerstone of semantics. For it is, as we just saw, fundamental to the learning of meaning. Also it is where meaning is firmest. The predicament of the indeterminacy of translation does not extend down to observation sentences. Sentences higher up in theories had no empirical consequences that they could call their own; but an observation sentence wears its empirical meaning on its sleeve. The equating of an observation sentence of our language to an observation sentence of another language is the merest matter of empirical generalization; it is a matter of identity between the range of stimulations that would prompt assent to the one sentence and the range of stimulations that would prompt assent to the other. This range of stimulations is, nearly enough, what I call the *stimulus meaning* of the sentence.

The observation sentence is a species of occasion sentence. An occasion sentence, in general, is one that we can assent to or dissent from only as prompted by a fresh stimulation

each time; thus 'This is cold,' 'That's a rabbit,' 'He's a bachelor,' 'It's raining.' They are unlike standing sentences, on
which one's verdict can stand for some time and simply be
repeated on demand. This contrast is really a matter of degree; thus even 'It's raining' stands for a while, and 'That's
a rabbit' and 'He's a bachelor' stand until the object of our
pointing gesture gets superseded. Still we may treat the occasion sentences roughly as a class. And the stimulus meaning
of an occasion sentence is, nearly enough, the class of those
stimulations that would prompt assent to it. Then an observation sentence, more particularly, is an occasion sentence
whose stimulus meaning is the same for all speakers. The
occasion sentence 'He's a bachelor' does not qualify as an
observation sentence, since different speakers will assent to
it under unlike confrontations; whether you recognize a man
as a bachelor is a variable accident of personal acquaintance.
On the other hand 'This is cold,' 'That's a rabbit,' and 'It's
raining' qualify pretty well as observation sentences—though
this quality again, like that of occasion sentence, could be
more strictly formulated as a matter of degree.

Stimulus meaning gives a fair account of meaning only
for observation sentences when different speakers are compared. But when we turn to comparing the stimulus meanings of different sentences for the same speaker, then, curi-
ously enough, we find that stimulus meaning gives a fair
account of meaning for occasion sentences generally. For any
one speaker, for instance, 'He's a bachelor' and 'He's an
unmarried man' have one and the same stimulus meaning—
even though each of these sentences has a different stimulus
meaning for each different speaker.

This circumstance can be exploited to define synonymy
for occasion sentences generally, and not only for one speaker
but over the community. We can equate 'He's a bachelor'
with 'He's an unmarried man' for the whole community, on

the ground that the two are synonymous for each speaker individually.

Only observation sentences could be equated between speakers by equating stimulus meaning. Still, by our indirect method we have transcended that limitation and defined community-wide synonymy for occasion sentences generally, observational and otherwise. By exploiting bilinguals we can press the same indirect method farther and define synonymy between occasion sentences even of different languages, without requiring them to be observation sentences. The indeterminacy of translation remains inescapable at higher levels, but our base is broader than the observation sentences.

Basic to all this there is the equating of stimulations. What is a stimulation? I argued in *Word and Object* that it should be a surface irritation, a triggering of receptors. Any peculiarities in the inner workings of a speaker are irrelevant to the social functioning of language, after all, as long as these peculiarities do not affect the relations between his stimulatory input and linguistic output as an interlocutor witnesses them. Events distant from the speaker's body are likewise irrelevant apart from their effects on the speaker.

So I construed the stimulation of a speaker on a given occasion as the class of those of his sensory receptors that are triggered on that occasion. But how then are we to equate the stimulations of two speakers for purposes of comparing their responses? Theoretically we should have to appeal to the triggering of corresponding receptors; and the trouble with this is the assumption that one person's sensory receptors are homologous, nerve by nerve, to another's. This is presumably false and anyway it surely ought not to have to matter. We should be free even to investigate the language of a visitor from one of the more exotic planets, despite the grotesque failure of that speaker's sensory receptors to pair up with our own.

Here is a striking irony. All this time we have been painfully warping ourselves over from a visionary phenomenalistic epistemology to the hardest-headed behaviorism, only to find at last that we cannot make sense of the hard-headed notion of stimulation itself.

Now Donald Davidson has lately pointed out to me that this whole homology difficulty can be by-passed simply by persisting in the dodge whereby, in *Word and Object,* I proposed to transcend observation sentences and define synonymy for all occasion sentences. As explained a few minutes ago, this dodge consisted in comparing and equating stimulus meanings for each speaker separately, intrasubjectively, and then integrating the results over the community by comparing the intrasubjective synonymies of one speaker with those of another. This procedure involves no comparing of stimulations of different speakers.

Davidson's observation is, at first impact, both comforting and unsettling. The locus of unsettlement is the observation sentence. Our definition of observation sentence did depend on comparing stimulations of different speakers; an observation sentence is one whose stimulus meaning is the same for all the speakers. But now the comparing of stimulations of different speakers is by-passed and so is the very notion of observation sentence. Cornerstone of semantics indeed.

This lecture has been a history of retreat from the most sanguine empiricism. Are we now to complete our withdrawal by giving up the notion of observation itself? No; what I lately said about its twofold importance still holds. First, the observation sentence is the repository of scientific evidence; second, it is the only avenue into a language, for the child and the field linguist alike. This is not belied by the discovery that we can frame a theory of synonymy and translation without the notion of observation sentence and without comparing different speakers' stimulations. That by-pass depended, in the case of translation, on the use of bilinguals. But in the pure field-linguistics case it is then the linguist himself who will have to go bilingual, having first broken his way into the native language by way as always of observation sentences; so these have their innings still, interesting though it is to see what a lot of theory can be made independent of the idea of them. As for defining observation sentences, perhaps that can still be managed without the embarrassment of having to equate different speakers' stimulations. The rough idea, after all, is just that observation sentences are the ones on which all members of the speech community give agreeing verdicts when in shared environments.

REFERENCES

Carnap, Rudolf. *Der logische Aufbau der Welt.* Berlin, 1928.
——— "Ueber Protokollsätze," Erkenntnis 3 (1932), pp. 215–228.
——— "Testability and meaning," Philosophy of Science 3 (1936), pp. 419–471; 4 (1937), pp. 1–40.
Hanson, N. R. "Observation and interpretation," Voice of America Forum Lecture, 1964. To appear in Sidney Morgenbesser, ed., *Philosophy of Science* (New York: Basic Books, 1966).
Johnson, A. B. *A Treatise on Language.* D. Rynin, ed. Berkeley: University of California, 1947.
Kuhn, T. S. *The Structure of Scientific Revolutions.* Chicago: University, 1962.
Neurath, Hans. "Protokollsätze," Erkenntnis 3 (1932), pp. 204–214.
Ogden, C. K. *Bentham's Theory of Fictions.* London, 1932.
Polanyi, Michael. *Personal Knowledge.* Chicago: University, 1958.
Quine, W. V. *Word and Object.* Cambridge, Mass.: M.I.T., 1960.
Russell, Bertrand. *Our Knowledge of the External World.* London, 1914.

J. O. Urmson

UTILITARIANISM

IT IS NOT CLEAR how close to the paradigm cases of Bentham and Mill an ethical position must be to count as a version of utilitarianism. It is not even always clear what question or questions philosophers who profess utilitarianism are setting themselves to answer. For these reasons, apart from any difficulties in the position, it would be bold to attempt a general defense of, or attack on, utilitarianism in a single lecture. More modestly, I shall first say a little, not very novel, to distinguish two importantly different projects on which moral theorists, including utilitarians, may embark. I shall then discuss some, but only some, of the different roles that rules may play in the making of moral decisions, in the belief that greater clarity about and discrimination of such rules is needed before we can profitably aim at the construction of any general utilitarian theory.

There are two enterprises, among others, in which utilitarians may be engaged which are very different in character. In the first place they may have raised the question: 'How in general ought we to decide problems of action?', and be constructing a general utilitarian theory in answer to this normative question. So viewed, utilitarianism is a very general moral proposal that we should decide all moral problems in terms of the utility of the various possible courses of action open; just how this is to be done will, no doubt, vary according to the detailed developments of the theory. Such a proposal is normative, is addressed to us as moral agents rather than as analysts or technical specialists, and should be defended as such. Thus G. E. Moore, who was engaged in an enterprise of this variety, rightly defended his version of utilitarianism in the last resort by appealing to the moral consciousness of his readers; could it, he asked, possibly ever be right to produce a lesser good or a greater evil in the world than it was in the agent's power to produce?

When utilitarianism is such a general moral proposal it is clearly of subsidiary importance, though not without interest, whether, and to what extent, the proposed utilitarian procedure coincides with the procedures in fact employed by people in coming to moral decisions. We are being invited to accept a procedure which may or may not resemble the procedures that we and others in fact employ. Presumably the questions most important to ask of such a utilitarian proposal are such as: 'Will it work?'; 'Would its use give acceptable answers to actual moral problems?'; 'Does it ask me to neglect considerations that seem to me of essential importance?'

Such a form of utilitarianism would have an analogue if a philosopher were to propose a method for settling scientific questions on the ground that it would be a rational and reliable method, whether or not it is in fact employed. But notoriously this is not the usual activity of students of scientific method. They make no claim to have devised a method, but rather that: (a) it is possible for us to recognize good and bad specimens of scientific procedure; (b) from the comparative examination of good specimens of scientific procedure it is possible to elicit a set of methodological principles implicit in them; (c) when examples of good scientific work do not manifestly exemplify this method they can be reconstructed without distortion so as to exemplify it. So these students of scientific method are addressing themselves to the question: 'What general methods of inquiry are exemplified, explicitly or implicitly, in what is recognizable, prior to philosophical investigation, as good scientific thinking?' They will be making no methodological proposals, good or bad, and the adequacy of their offering must be tested by comparing their account of scientific method with actual practice and seeing to what degree it faithfully illuminates it.

I think that some utilitarians are addressing themselves to a question similar to that about scientific method which has just been sketched. They claim that we can distinguish, prior to philosophical reflection, good from bad pieces of moral thinking; we do not need philosophy to tell us that it is a good reason for giving a person special consideration that he is ill, a bad reason for so doing that he was born on March 4th. Their problem is then to construct a general utilitarian thesis which will play a role with regard to moral thinking analogous to that which a theory of scientific method plays with regard to good scientific thinking. Their utilitarianism will be a general account of the principles implicit in good moral thnking as we find it.

There is, no doubt, the risk that in this sort of work moral philosophers will allow their theories to bias their judgment of good and bad samples of moral thinking; the same danger exists in the study of scientific method. But if such a utilitarian thesis is offered we do not in this case have to ask whether it would be morally acceptable to us as the primary consideration in weighing its adequacy. Rather we must compare the theory with examples of ordinary good moral practice and consider how illuminatingly and accurately it portrays them. Now our theoretical acumen is challenged, rather than our moral insight.

The two types of inquiry just distinguished are not by

any means always clearly discriminated by their practitioners. Which for example, if either, is exemplified by the work of Bentham and Mill? Yet it is essential to know if critical reflection is to be appropriate. Though they should be distinguished they may be combined; a utilitarian may, for example, believe that more than one procedure is commonly accepted for solving moral issues and regard his version of utilitarianism as faithfully exhibiting one while he rejects others as, in his view, morally inadequate. Thus we shall have a combination of moral advocacy and theoretical analysis.

Having distinguished these two types of inquiry, for the rest of this paper we shall be concerned with utilitarianism only in so far as it is the more analytical version. Such a utilitarianism must take notice of the actual facts of moral thinking as we find it.

Now if we glance even cursorily at these facts we cannot but notice that frequently, though not always, an explicit appeal is made to a general rule of conduct, to some principle, in the determination of a concrete moral issue. Moreover, these rules or principles cannot plausibly be regarded as versions of a general principle of utility. So utilitarianism must give some account of the place of rules, other than the principle of utilitarianism itself, in moral deliberation. Rules such as those prohibiting lying, stealing, promise breaking, malice and treachery do play some part in our moral thinking. What can a utilitarian say about them?

Now (notoriously in philosophical circles) there are two types of utilitarianism distinguished by the account they give of the status of such rules. Schematically they are (1) act-utilitarianism, which claims that these rules play only a heuristic role, that they are all but rules of thumb, useful to remember in doubtful or difficult situations or when time is too short adequately to determine one's course of action by the sole authoritative utilitarian principle; (2) rule-utilitarianism, which claims that these rules play an essential role, that they are authoritative in particular moral situations, though they must be established and justified in the light of the supreme utilitarian principle. These schematic outlines do not, of course, do justice to the views of any actual philosopher. Thus G. E. Moore is often classified, not without justification, as an act-utilitarian. Yet he asserts most categorically in *Principia Ethica* that there are a number of moral rules other than the utilitarian principle which we can never be justified in breaking (e.g., Para. 99).

But, though these schematic accounts of act- and rule-utilitarianism are admittedly over-simple, it does seem to me that neither the proponents nor the opponents of utilitarianism, in either of its forms, have given adequate attention to the great variety of functions that rules can play in practical thinking. In making some attempt now to discriminate three types of rules I am trying to provide data for a more sophisticated account of the place of moral rules in our thinking than either act- or rule-utilitarianism usually offers. I am not under the impression that there are only these three types— far from it, but there is not time for a more exhaustive examination of rules now, were I capable of it.

I propose, then, to distinguish three types of general moral principles amongst the many that can, I believe, be discerned. My first type is the familiar rule of thumb.

1. RULES OF THUMB

Typical examples of rules of thumb from non-moral contexts would be (in the game of bridge) 'Third hand plays high' or (in chess) 'Do not move the same piece twice in the opening'. These rules clearly have a different status and function from the rules of bridge or of chess, proper. They are legion in the practical affairs of life—'Always lock your car when it is unattended'; 'ne'er cast a clout till May is out';

'clean your teeth night and morning'; and so forth. Such rules are based on factual observations of the kind: 'over and over again the best play for the third player is a high card' or: 'over and over again moving the same piece twice in the opening leads to a retarded development'. The justification of a rule of thumb is then that if you cannot see with fair certainty that something else is better it will be prudent to do the thing that usually is best. When something else obviously is better, to follow the rule of thumb would be merely stupid; we should not even follow the rule in such situations in order to encourage others to conform to the rule, for we do not wish to encourage others to conform to the rule in such situations. Again, while the rule of bridge that the dealer bids first is authoritative—its existence is in itself a reason why the dealer should bid first—the rule of thumb is not authoritative; its existence is not a *reason why,* say, third hand should play high, though it may be a *reason for believing* that third hand should play high in many situations.

There is no reason to doubt that some rules quoted in moral contexts are of this kind. There are many wise saws in the didactic books of the Old Testament which should surely be construed as of this character rather than as appendices to the ten commandments. They present no serious difficulties to any utilitarian, for the rule-utilitarian need not claim that *no* rules are merely rules of thumb. But it is more difficult to see how the utilitarian who claims to regard the actual facts of moral thinking can plausibly reduce all principles of just, honorable and fair dealing to this category.

There are then rules of thumb. They are of mere heuristic value. That there exists such a rule is not in itself a reason why one should conform to it, though it may be wise to conform to it in some circumstances and it may be a reason for believing that one should act in a certain way on some occasions.

I next distinguish

2. RULES CONSTITUTIVE OF AN END

Aristotle, or, let us say, the author of the *Magna Moralia,* says that happiness is composed of certain activities which are constitutive of it, and that happiness is nothing over and above these activities. The contemplation of the divine, for example, is not a means to happiness but the most important ingredient in happiness itself. This is, I think, a clue for the understanding of the place of certain rules; let us start with a non-moral example. Let us suppose that a group of us join together to form a club, the end or aim of which is the promotion of the arts. We might need to agree on a set of rules, which would include rules about subscriptions, meeting times and places, election of officers and the like. Such rules as these will be justified, if justifiable at all, on the ground that the conduct they prescribe will be a means, however humble, to the end for which the club exists; such conduct will have no independent value. But the very first rule might well be something like this: 'Each member shall himself practice some art, shall support artistic projects and encourage education in the arts'. But such conduct as this is not a means to, subservient to, the promotion of the arts; the rule prescribes the kind of conduct which constitutes the promotion of the arts. Moreover, if we neglect to follow this rule, we are not neglecting to follow some useful rule of thumb by following which we are more likely to promote the arts; we are simply failing to promote the arts. This rule would be an example of what I call a rule constitutive of an end.

Something analogous may, I think, hold in the case of morality. Let us suppose that each of us has some picture, no doubt fragmentary and even, perhaps, not wholly consistent, of what he wishes the world in general to be like. A utilitarian will regard the realization of the picture, so far as is possible, as the goal of moral action. Now in so far as

I have such a picture it certainly includes not merely people having certain pleasant feelings but also certain relationships holding between people. In other words, certain relationships between people seem to be worthwhile in themselves, of intrinsic value, and not merely conducive to what has intrinsic value. Personal relationships having a plausible claim to such a status are kindness, candor and good faith, though no doubt they also have a value as means to other intrinsically valuable things. It is then plausible to regard moral rules enjoining kindness, candor and good-faith as rules partially constitutive of an end, the general good, rather than as only productive of this end. We ought, for example, to be in good faith with our neighbors at least partly because such a relationship is in itself a thing of value. If that is so, a rule enjoining good faith can clearly not be classified as a rule of thumb.

Such rules partially constitutive of an end are not to be confused with moral principles of the kind depicted by such philosophers as Ross and Prichard, called by the technically-minded 'deontologists.' I am not saying that the rightness of certain acts is independent of their consequences, that duties can be simply seen to be such and must be done because they are duties without further ado, that justice must prevail though the heavens fall. Such a view is intended to be a denial of utilitarianism. I am saying rather that certain rules may require certain actions as duties because the action is itself of value as an end; that certain rules should be obeyed, not even if the heavens should fall, but because people acting in this way is part of what it is for the heavens to stand. To lay down a principle requiring conduct of a certain kind and to offer as the reason that such conduct is itself of value is as little a pleonasm, is as much informative, as to offer as the reason that such conduct *produces* what is of value. The recognition of such rules is perfectly *compatible* with at least some versions of utilitarianism, though it does not of course *require* a rigid utilitarianism.

To guard against possible misunderstanding, let me add that when I suggest that a certain kind of action may be enjoined by a rule because action of that kind is regarded as partially constitutive of the end I am in no way suggesting that the end must be regarded as wholly constituted by actions of a certain kind, that the end is the sum total of actions partly constitutive of it. I am not denying that classical utilitarianism is right in regarding certain states of feeling as being in themselves of value. I am suggesting that classical utilitarianism was wrong in holding that *only* certain states of consciousness are of value in themselves and that actions can be only of instrumental value. I see no sound reason for supposing that mankind does, or should, find intrinsic value only in states of consciousness; there is no need to go to the opposite extreme of denying value to states of consciousness. In suggesting that acting in good faith, for example, may be partially constitutive of the end, I wish to imply that we should think of it, as well as pleasure and the absence of pain, as having the sort of status in moral thinking allowed by classical utilitarianism only to pleasure and the absence of pain; it will be thought of as having the same kind of value as pleasure and the absence of pain.

The third type of rule I shall mention is:

3. RULES ALLOCATING RESPONSIBILITIES

These rules determine who is primarily responsible for carrying out certain tasks. Obvious examples are rules laying down duties stemming from social relationships. I have no great store of anthropological and sociological learning, but it is surely clear that, depending on the type of social organization, such rules as these vary noticeably between different cultural groups. Moreover while we may find the moral institutions of some cultural groups abhorrent to us in various respects, it seems that we cannot claim an inherent superiority for any one set of moral institutions over all others. Thus in most modern western countries we should acknowledge a duty of care towards aged or infirm parents to lie on their children, both sons and daughters; but in a nomadic patriarchal society, where the wife joins the husband's family, it may be quite reasonably the case that after marriage she is thought to have no special duty of care towards her parents, but only towards her husband's. To oversimplify and exaggerate a little, we may say that what matters is that the moral institutions ensure that the aged and infirm are cared for, and that just how this is done will legitimately vary according to the conditions of life that obtain.

Such rules as these determining our moral responsibilities to our fellow-men seem to be quite unlike rules of thumb; they are injunctions and prohibitions which determine the structure of our society rather than tips about what is most likely to improve the world. They are more like a moral rule of the road than tips on good driving, and, like the rule of the road, should be obeyed as the alternative to chaos even if one thinks them capable of improvement. The moral chaos which ensued when the missionaries, aided by the British government, put an end to the polygamous marriage practices and the moral code that went with them in certain South Sea Islands can be painfully discovered in Sir Arthur Gimble's book, *A Return to the Islands*. But, if not mere rule-of-thumb tips, neither are such moral rules as these in important respects similar to the rules constitutive of the end which we previously noticed. We might well think it wise and good to conform to their institutional morality when visiting people of a different culture, and in so doing should not have significantly changed our basic moral outlook, whereas to abandon rules constitutive of the end is to make a fundamental change in one's moral outlook. If these people hold it reprehensible to speak to a strange woman, then perhaps we should not do so; but if they were to indulge in certain barbaric cruelties, we need not think ourselves licensed to do so also.

We have now distinguished three types of moral rule, the heuristic, non-authoritative, rule of thumb, the rule partially constitutive of the end and the institutional rule delimiting responsibilities. I am very far from believing that this is an exhaustive list of types of moral rule. Thus I have quite deliberately omitted any mention of universal rules enjoining or prohibiting certain actions which we might treat as mandatory and authoritative rather than as rules of thumb because of the danger of permitting exceptions or because of our fallibility in recognizing exceptions, though this is probably the favorite example of orthodox rule-utilitarians from the jurisprudent Austin onwards.

The three types of rule I have distinguished are, I hope, clear enough to make the intended points of this paper, the first of which is quite simply that there can be no *single* answer to the question of the place of moral rules in practical deliberation. But it would be very desirable (a worthwhile Ph.D. project) to attempt a more exhaustive discrimination than any we now have time for.

I wish now to raise the question, so worrying to utilitarians, of when and why we may make exceptions to moral rules, in the light of the recognition that they may fulfil quite different functions. But first we must make some general points about exceptions to rules without special reference to moral issues.

(1) If a rule really is a heuristic rule of thumb, a prudential maxim, there is no question of *making* an exception to it, but rather of *finding* and observing the limits of its scope. The rule tells us that in circumstances Y it is usually the case that it is best to do X and that thus there is an *a priori* likelihood that it will be best to do X on any given occasion. If, as third player at bridge, one does not play high, one's partner may with reason complain on a certain occasion that

one had no reason to think that the rule of thumb did not
then hold good; but if there are manifest reasons for playing
low the heuristic maxim has not even a slight weight to the
contrary. The existence of an authoritative rule is in itself a
reason, if not always a sufficient one, for acting as the rule
lays down; quite otherwise in the case of heuristic rules of
thumb.

(2)   When we have an authoritative rule we must
distinguish our making an exception to, or breaking, the
rule from the rule itself admitting, perhaps even specifying,
exceptions. This distinction can be rather trivially illustrated
as follows: if there is a rule 'keep off the grass' then if I ever
walk on the grass I break, or make an exception to, the rule;
but if the rule is 'keep off the grass except on Sundays', then,
if I walk on the grass on Sunday, I take advantage of the
specified exception and do not break the rule. Now, though
this distinction is clear and simple, philosophers often blur
it. Thus they seem sometimes to be inclined to argue that
such moral rules as those prohibiting lying, promise-breaking
or stealing must have implicit exceptions built into them
because lying, promise-breaking and stealing can sometimes
be justified. But this does not follow. If there is a rule 'keep
off the grass' but I see an old lady fall over on the far side
of it, I am no doubt justified in running across the grass to
her. But is it not the case that I am now justified in *breaking*
the rule rather than that what the park authority really meant
was something like 'keep off the grass except when necessary
to relieve suffering, obviate danger' etc., etc.? I will not plead
that I have not broken the rule but that I was justified in
doing so. Similarly, if I break a fairly trivial promise in order
to relieve serious suffering, surely I *have* broken my promise,
justifiably, rather than taken advantage of one of an amor-
phous list of unstated escape-clauses? Still less can a rule-
utilitarian allow that all moral rules have attached to them
an implicit escape-clause 'unless better consequences would

follow from acting otherwise'. For if that were so all moral rules of the form 'In circumstances Y, do X' would be reduced to the injunction to do whatever has the best consequences —the basic utilitarian principle—with the trivial exception that, if the consequences of doing X in circumstances Y are exactly as good as those of the best alternative, one should do X.

No doubt rules *may* have implicit escape-clauses. But that it is in general a mistake to regard moral rules in this way seems to me clear from the fact that a departure from their explicit injunction is always hazardous and a matter for regret. If John Doe breaks a trivial promise to Richard Roe with justification, he should still regret having broken it and an apology is due. If there were an escape-clause, then the promise would not really have been broken and regrets and apologies would be misplaced. Why should one feel compunction about doing what the rule specifically permits or even commands? But which ever way we regard any particular case, there surely is a difference between making a justified breach of a rule and taking advantage of an escape-clause and it deserves more careful recognition in moral philosophy.

If, then, we allow that there are authoritative moral rules, other than some supreme utilitarian principle, it is notoriously a hard problem for the rule-utilitarian to state how we can and do determine when and if the breach of one of them is justified. Indeed many critics have alleged that this cannot be done; more than one critic has produced arguments purporting to show that rule-utilitarianism must, when pushed on this matter, either cease to be utilitarian or collapse into act-utilitarianism. What I wish to suggest, one main proposition of this paper, is that only when we have distinguished the very different roles that rules can play in moral thinking can we begin profitably to raise the question when exceptions can be made to them. I have sketchily suggested three roles in this paper. I now say that it can only be after a much fuller study of such distinctions has been made that a rule-utilitarian can usefully present his case. Let me finally give some inadequate illustrations of this point in the light of the few distinctions we have noted.

There is clearly no problem about rules of thumb. We have seen that they are heuristic, neither mandatory nor authoritative, and so it is wrong to speak of breaches of them even when we fail to follow them. We may make an error of judgment and unwisely disregard one, but this error is that of failing to make proper use of available data, not a breach of rule.

If we turn now to rules that I have called partially constitutive of an end we can see that this very feature of them makes a decisive difference when the question of a possible breach arises. If there be such rules, and I think that there are, then clearly it could not be the case ever that *this time* doing the reverse of what the rule enjoins would be in itself preferable to following it, as might well be the case given rules of a different status. For if we regard acting in good faith as in itself part of the good to be aimed at how could acting in bad faith ever be in itself preferable? Again, if a situation arises where two rules constitutive of the end conflict (and there is no reason to suppose the world to be so comfortably arranged that candor, say, can never conflict with kindness), then surely, in the case of rules of *this* kind, the prime consideration in deciding which to follow and which to break may well be a direct assessment of the value of the competing courses of action in the present context, though this decision procedure might be quite inapplicable to conflicts of other types of rule.

This simple decision procedure would be plainly inapplicable to such rules as delimit primary responsibilities. Such rules seem to be a classic case for the familiar utilitarian argument that one reason for obeying a rule is just the maintenance of its authority. Since a prime point of such rules is that they determine who is responsible for seeing that various socially necessary things get done by someone, considerations quite other than that of the value of any single action in conformity with them must arise with regard to their observances, such as their relative importance for social stability.

Inevitably, therefore, a possible clash between a rule constitutive of an end and one delimiting primary responsibilities must be one which raises quite new considerations. Indeed a simple case of such a clash will rarely arise. For one feature of rules determining primary responsibilities is that they partially determine the content of rules constitutive of ends. Thus if unkindness is something that we can regard as in itself bad irrespective of its, no doubt, evil consequences, an act may become an act of this sort just because it involves a breach of a rule determining responsibility; my failure to devote special attention to somebody might, for example, be unkind just because the special attention was owed, but would not be otherwise. It seems obvious, then, that different problems are involved when there is a simple conflict between a rule constitutive of an end and a rule determining responsibilities and such a conflict when it gives rise to a conflict of rules constitutive of ends.

So different considerations will arise when we have (1) a clash of rules constitutive of ends; (2) a clash of rules determining primary responsibilities; (3) a clash between rules of each of these kinds. Since there are undoubtedly also rules of morality of still other types it is no wonder that critics of utilitarianism have found the simple decision procedures offered by utilitarians as general accounts of how to justify the making of exceptions to rules much too simple. The facts of morality are complex, and utilitarianism must become much more complex if it is to deal with them. We would be oversimplifying if we assumed that all moral problems involve an appeal to rules, though some do; it is the diversity of these rules that I have been emphasizing.

One final point of no small importance. Critics of utilitarianism have, not without reason, noted another point at which the utilitarian account of rules and their function has been unclear and inconsistent. Sometimes, these critics point out, the rules appear to be thought of as existing, accepted, norms; it is when they have been so represented that the question of setting a good example, of maintaining respect for the moral code, has seemed important; at other times the utilitarian represents himself as following rules which are to be justified because their observation would maximize well-being, whether or not they are observed in any particular society. Utilitarianism has, indeed, been vague and unclear on this point. But it seems that here too greater precision and clarity can be achieved by the recognition of the varying force of moral rules. Thus the rules determining primary responsibilities that we have been considering surely do largely acquire their force from being generally accepted; that is at least part of their value. We might think them improvable and attempt to have those recognized in our society modified; but what is recognized in fact must largely determine where our special responsibilities lie. But with rules constitutive of an end the case is far otherwise; if good faith, for example, seems to us to be of value in itself, then we should surely follow the rule of good faith whether or not others recognize it. Thus the utilitarian ought not to be vague; but his vacillation in the past is readily intelligible once we see that the realization of the variety of rules requires us sometimes to emphasize, sometimes to neglect, the question whether the rules in question are publicly recognized.

I do not say that utilitarianism is right or wrong. I do say that past versions of it have been much too simple and have been open to justified criticism on the ground of vagueness and inadequacy. We need to devise more complicated versions of it; not surprisingly, since moral life is complicated. It may well be that the more complicated versions will also be inadequate; we cannot know without looking to see. In this lecture I have been programmatically indicating that one way in which utilitarianism needs to become more complicated is by the recognition of and delineation of a far wider variety of rules of conduct than in the past and by study of how the different types of rules will be differently treated in moral deliberation. I have tried to give a few examples of how this further study might proceed, but they have been only sketchy examples; the work remains to be done. I would further lay special emphasis on the study of rules constitutive of ends; if a clear and satisfactory account of such rules can be given, many of the standard objections to utilitarianism as inadequate to the moral facts might, perhaps, be obviated. In any case I am sure that the study of moral thinking, though old in years, is still childlike in its simplicity; so utilitarianism, like other moral theories, has been neither vindicated nor refuted. We must see what we can make of it rather than attack or defend the primitive sketches so far available.

Stuart Hampshire

AESTHETICS

AS THE

MIDDLE GROUND

I WISH IN THIS LECTURE to take a step outside the normal confines of analytical philosophy and to make an experiment in the phenomenology of aesthetic experience, an experiment that was suggested to me by Kant's *Critique of Judgment*. In discriminating the value attached to different kinds of experience, the final appeal must be to the individual's consciousness of his own sentiments and attitudes, as he experiences them, and to his acknowledgment after reflection of the fittingness of a suggested description. The warrant of truthfulness can only be that a significant number of readers will be inclined, on reflection, to say: "I recognize the appropriateness of this description; your, or Kant's, formulations, strained and unusual as they may be, do reproduce some of the considerations that I obscurely have in mind when I try to distinguish this one kind of enjoyment from other kinds. Your description is at least one accurate way, as far as my experience goes, of picking out some of the salient features of aesthetic experience."

Kant tried to explain the importance attributed to the arts, and to the enjoyment of art, in relation to morality and to

the scientific and philosophical interests of men. Taking the
three critiques together, he offers a system from which a
phenomenology of the enjoyment of art, and of aesthetic enjoyment generally, can, by selection, be extracted. It happens
that the descriptions that he suggests of the peculiar features
of this enjoyment seem to me more penetrating, and closer
to my experience, than any others known to me. Yet his
own interest in the arts seems to have been relatively super-
ficial and casual. He disliked music; he had seen very little
original painting; his taste in literature was largely the conventional taste of his time. But the system led him to observations which seem to me to constitute the best available
beginning of discussion.

There is no need, for the purposes of this lecture, to
examine once again Kant's account of moral reasoning. It is
sufficient for our purposes that we should understand Kant's
distinction between men's conception of themselves as free
agents, whose freedom is an overcoming of the impulses and
interests attributable to natural causes, and their conception
of themselves as fit subjects for scientific study and understanding no less than other objects in nature. The tension
between these two conceptions of himself in relation to the
natural order, which each man necessarily has, produces
that strain and conflict which we call the sense of duty, and
so produces morality. We recognize that we are dealing with
a moral question just in virtue of recognizing that the natural
laws that govern human desire and feeling are in conflict at
a certain point with the laws that our reason prescribes for
rational beings. The central concept here is that of nature,
in the eighteenth century sense; that is, of an orderly and
lawful succession of observable phenomena which we can
learn to anticipate and to control by penetrating to the simple
structure beneath the phenomena. But it had been suggested
that our control, where our own sentiments and interests are
in question, amounts to following the laws self-consciously,

and without confusion of mind, which we would have followed unself-consciously and uncertainly, if we had not been enlightened: or so the men of the Enlightenment believed. For them our moral enlightenment consists only in being aware of the laws of human psychology in their full generality. But Kant reverses the dictum of the Enlightenment, and particularly of Hume, that morality consists in following our nature, fully understood. On the contrary, morality, that is, rational freedom, consists in looking beyond one's given and ascertainable nature towards an ideal world. To act as a free man acts is to act against one's given and ascertainable natural disposition. A dual, or ambiguous, attitude to nature is forced upon one whenever one takes a decision to act in a particular way in the light of facts about oneself which one knows and which one might explain scientifically. One first accepts the facts with the understanding and then rejects them with the will. The natural order is necessarily adapted to our understanding of it, and at the same time our reason, recognizing this necessity, will press questions about its own powers, and will make demands, which cannot be answered, and cannot be met, by any conceivable observation of nature.

The place of aesthetic experience is on a middle ground between the scientific understanding of the natural order and the moral demand that we should think of ourselves as prescribing an ideal order of our own. If there were not this middle ground, we would be in a state of irresoluble conflict. There would be no connection between the purely rational ideal of what our nature should be and our observation of what it in fact is. There would be no continuity between our observation of our behavior and environment, and our evaluation of our behavior and environment as falling short of a standard that we, as rational beings, have prescribed. But in fact our language shows that there is such a connection and continuity. There is a clearly marked class of judgments which are both descriptions of objects observed and also evaluations of them. It is not true that, for clear thinking and in an ideal language, we should never combine in a single predicate an evaluation and a description of something observed, as many empiricists have suggested. We *must* combine them, if we are not to be torn apart by a Platonic conflict between rationality on the one hand, and emotion and the senses on the other. If music is to be thought of as mathematics clothed in sound, the beauty resides at the point of contact, or fitting, between the sensuous clothing and the rational structure, when this fitting seems entirely natural. Similarly, when we observe the mechanism of our body in action as a physical phenomenon, we can see the adaptation of the parts of the body in the whole movement as perfect or imperfect; therefore we see not only the neutrally statable facts about the movement, but the quality or excellence of it also. In the ordinary employment of the senses we see natural objects and processes as exhibiting purposes in their perceptible forms: rhythms, patterns, orders of intervals, which we may neglect for purposes of scientific understanding under concepts, but which satisfy the imagination in synthesizing perceptions. If we suspend our normal curiosity, and the need to subsume our percepts under concepts, we may look at natural objects and artefacts simply as spectacles, more or less well adapted to this non-cognitive interest. Then the faculty of the imagination is set free to play upon its proper objects, and is the source of a peculiar type of judgment, which is a judgment of the physiognomy of things, as beautiful or ugly in a great variety of ways. What, according to Kant, are the marks of this class of judgments?

But "let us forget"—you may interrupt at this point, following the spirit of the times—"the demands of his system-building, and any question-begging apparatus of philosophical terms; let us first regard the facts, the variegated idioms of our speech, which are the repository of the common sense of mankind. Let us examine what we ordinarily mean by a work of art, and how works of art are ordinarily appraised in a multitude of quite different ways. Then we shall at least be on firm ground, and can start safely from there, if we are to theorize about the relation of art and aesthetic experience to morality." On the contrary, it now seems to me that we would be on hopelessly shifting ground. And this for two connected reasons. First, to mark the proper domain either of ethics (moral judgment) or of aesthetics always has been, and necessarily always will be, to declare a particular, and disputable, moral or aesthetic theory, in the sense in which a "theory" is an arguable opinion, and certainly is not a teachable rule, or a convention of valid argument, or of correct speech. Let a contemporary philosopher say, for example, in pseudo-Aristotelian manner, that the domain of ethics is the domain of action and practical choice. Such a statement, or (worse) assumption, is a wilful and opinionated judgment which has consequences that are more than methodological. Who is to exclude, and upon what authority, the range of attitudes, feelings, impulses, inclinations and emotions, even thoughts, that do not issue in action, as belonging to another domain, their goodness or evil to be discussed in other terms and by arguments of a different pattern? Of course some grounds *can* be found in common speech for such an exclusion, for drawing *a* line, or *the* line, just as these points, separating action and feeling: but grounds can also be found in common speech, over the centuries, for drawing a line to mark the domain of ethics and aesthetics elsewhere. And this leads to my second reason for looking to the system-builder: in any case we have to begin from some division of human interests, activities, powers, and it is less confusing to begin with a division that is entirely explicit and deliberately explained and introduced, rather than from a division that has been tacitly assumed or taken for granted. What exactly counts as action and what is contemplation? Is imagination a moral faculty? By what criterion shall we decide, and

whence comes the authority of any criterion proposed? And
if we say that a man ought to develop his powers of imagination, is this the so-called moral "ought"? Is this a moral
judgment? Are independence of mind and judgment, and
originality, moral virtues? How are we to decide? We cannot
read off the answers from the shared habits of common
speech, unless we are prepared to accept conventional judgments of value unchallenged. It is therefore not unreason-
able at least to start from a philosophical conception of the
human mind, one that is designed all in one piece, that tries
systematically to show the place of art in human life, within
the whole range of practical and theoretical interests. Then
it is possible to see at what points one would oneself, and
as a clear-sighted decision, wish to amend, and greatly to
complicate, this philosophical reconstruction, or perhaps why
one would wish to reject it altogether at certain points.

We must not then simply assume from the beginning that
there is a single domain of aesthetic interests, where this is
the assumption that there is something both common *and*
peculiar to our interest in art and to our interest in natural
beauty, including in natural beauty observed features of human behavior. There *may* be something both common and
peculiar to these two human interests, which importantly
marks them off from all others, so that what is common is
more fundamental than what is different. Kant certainly
thought that this was so; he thought that there is a distinguish-
able class of pure aesthetic judgments which may refer either
to human creations or to natural things, and that a formed
critical estimate of a work of art is, among other things, a
pure aesthetic judgment. And the wide use of this very term
was new, introduced by Baumgarten in the same century, and
the word brought with it a new conception of the liberal, or
free, arts as constituting a separate domain of enjoyment in
perception. Within the class of aesthetic judgments Kant still
made important distinctions between those which refer to

natural objects, and those which refer to human creations, and which are the expressions of talent or genius.

One may in the end find grounds for denying that an interest in art is always and necessarily one and the same as an interest in beauty, or in the sublime, and that works of art can be characterized merely as a species of the genus beautiful or sublime things, namely, those beautiful or sublime things which are the products of human genius, imaginatively imitating nature in the expression of aesthetic ideas. It is the danger of the very recognition of a subject-matter of aesthetics that it may seem to carry too many implications with it: it carries the implication that there is a clearly marked class of aesthetic judgments, which includes judgments of sensuous beauty and judgments of works of art, and that there is a corresponding faculty of taste which is equally the source of our enjoyment of beautiful things and of our appraisal of works of art. It is then only a short step to the conclusion that, in the enjoyment and appraisal of works of art, one is primarily interested in some relations of form in the process of sense-perception: perhaps also that these relations can be abstracted from the particular intentions, the peculiar sensibility and the communicated feelings, of their makers; all these are assumptions to be challenged and to be tested by appeal to our own experience.

There is one more preliminary point of method. The principles of Kant's philosophy require that all philosophical questions about the nature of art, and of our interest in it, should be re-formulated as questions about the distinguishing features of a particular kind of judgment, or, if you prefer, proposition. Philosophy, as opposed to psychology and any of the natural sciences, was for Kant the examination of the peculiar implications, the peculiar logical force, the peculiar claims made, by a particular kind of judgment, marked off by the method of confirmation that is distinctively appropriate to it. His examination is systematic and legislative, in the sense that it depends upon a general scheme of the types of possible judgment. This general scheme is a distillation from distinctions in methods of confirmation that are marked by distinct idioms in common speech; but they are not constantly and invariably marked. So he arrives at a pure form of judgment, empirical, moral, aesthetic, which does not always appear in its appropriate pure form in the carelessness of ordinary speech. When Kant says that all aesthetic judgments make a claim to necessity, he means that he will not count as a genuine case of a pure valid aesthetic judgment any utterance that does not have the force of claiming to be binding on all men. A person may unreflectingly think that he is appraising something as a work of art, and what he says may, in its form of expression, look or sound like an aesthetic judgment; but it will not count as a genuine one, unless it satisfies the conditions of confirmation which Kant distinguishes as peculiar to this type in its pure, canonical form. Kant of course looks for confirmation of his defining conditions of aesthetic judgment in the habits of ordinary discourse; but he does not trouble with apparent counter-examples. His reasons for prescribing these conditions for the type are to be found in his systematic classification of the whole range of possible human judgments. Confusion between the different types, assuming that one is committing oneself to one type of judgment when it emerges in cross-examination that one is in fact making another type of judgment, is the most common source of error in aesthetics, as in ethics. The principal service of philosophy is to save us from this type of unreflective confusion: to enable us to disentangle scientific issues from metaphysical issues, moral questions from technical questions, matters of critical appraisal in aesthetics from expressions of personal taste. Then we will always be self-conscious and clearly aware of what we are committing ourselves to.

An entirely pure aesthetic judgment is a judgment typically expressed in the words "This is, or was, beautiful," and this form of words has not been correctly used to make a pure aesthetic judgment unless all of the following conditions are satisfied:

(1) That the man making the judgment has actually derived pleasure from the mere contemplation or apprehension of the object referred to. A sentence has not been correctly used to convey a pure aesthetic judgment unless the speaker or writer intends to assert that he himself takes pleasure in the mere contemplation of the object referred to. For instance, it is not an aesthetic judgment if the speaker says only that the object is of a kind that ordinarily affords him pleasure in the mere contemplation of it, or of a kind that ordinarily affords most people pleasure in the mere contemplation of it.

(2) A *pure* aesthetic judgment must be singular, both in the sense that it refers to a particular object—or presumably aggregate of particular objects—and in the sense that it does not commit the speaker to any general proposition that goes beyond his own actual perceptions, past and present. I am not in a position to make a genuine aesthetic judgment about any object with which I am not myself directly acquainted. And so no judgment which I would defend, if challenged, by an appeal to inference or induction could be a genuine aesthetic judgment.

(3) No pure aesthetic judgment is susceptible of any kind of proof or demonstration. The only method—if it can be called a method—by which its truth or validity can be tested is by critical reflection. And the point of the critical reflection is to ensure that the pleasure reported really is pleasure in the mere contemplation of the object and not pleasure of some other kind. I must reflect to be sure that I have abstracted from the factors which may contingently affect my estimate of the object.

These three conditions, very roughly stated, give the sense in which we might be inclined to call aesthetic judgments subjective,—subjective, certainly, in comparison with moral judgments, which have to be strictly universal in form, and to contain no reference to any particular thing, person, or occasion. It is to be observed that, as far as these three conditions alone are concerned, aesthetic judgments could be a peculiar kind of avowal or autobiographical statement, with so far nothing normative about them.

But condition (4) is: any genuine aesthetic judgment claims that everyone else ought to agree with the speaker in his estimate of the object referred to, and therefore in feeling the pleasure in the contemplation of the object which is the ground of this estimate. It is one of the implications of a pure aesthetic judgment that, in Kant's phrase, the speaker is "a suitor for agreement from everyone else, because he is fortified with a ground common to all." And this introduces condition (5) of a judgment being counted as a pure aesthetic judgment: that the pleasure reported should not be pleasure in the existence of the object referred to, or associated with any interest in, or desire for, it which the speaker happens to have, but should be a pleasure solely in the speaker's manner of apprehending or being aware of it. A pure aesthetic judgment claims that the speaker, in making his estimate, has altogether disregarded any particular interest that he may have in this particular object's existence, or in the existence of objects of this kind, or any appeal to his emotions which are associated with its existence. Kant of course has to insist that this distinction between kinds of pleasure *is* a distinction between kinds of pleasure, and not a distinction between the psychological causes of pleasure. Otherwise the judgment could not be immediate and singular, but would be causal and inductive, and therefore empirical. That is why I have used the form "pleasure *in* our manner of apprehension." The claim implies that we can know directly, after careful reflection, whether our pleasure is a pleasure in the object existing and being the kind of object that it is, or whether it is a pleasure in some satisfying harmony in our manner of apprehending the object, a pleasure which recurs, in spite of other variable factors, in such a way as to show that the object is perfectly adapted to our mode of apprehension. If it is the second, then the ground of the pleasure is something that should be common to everybody; it is not a pleasure in, or enjoyment of, the emotional charm, the emotional appeal, the particular associations, that the object has for one person and might not have for another. The aesthetic judgment claims that the pleasure in the harmony of faculties of apprehension will *necessarily* be felt by anyone who, in contemplation of the object, is not distracted by other interests. If two people disagree in making judgments which, in their manner of expression, both claim to be pure aesthetic judgments, it must be true that at least one of them is mistaken in this claim; he, or perhaps both of them, are confusing a pleasure in the existence of the object, or of some of the features of it, with a pure aesthetic pleasure, that is, pleasure in the free play of the imagination that the apprehension of it involves. At least one of them is making what Kant calls an erroneous aesthetic judgment, saying "This is beautiful" when he should have said "This is charming, or is attractive to me, or this has some pleasant associations for me, or this stirs my emotions." In any pure aesthetic enjoyment of an object, whatever it may be, appetite and will are suspended, and the curiosity that serves them, the desire to know more about the thing as the effect of causes, is suspended also.

There are many important obscurities here which you will no doubt want to question: for instance, what is the *necessity* of common agreement, which is distinguished from the mere psychological fact that everyone does agree, or from the empirical hypothesis that, if they were not distracted by other interests, they would agree? Secondly, what is meant by the implicit claim that everyone *ought* to agree in their judgment, because the satisfying harmony in the mode of apprehension of a beautiful object *must* be common to all men? But for our purposes now it will be enough to indicate what kind of ac-

count is suggested of the importance of art, and of the enjoyment of natural beauty. First, it requires that both the enjoyment and aesthetic estimation of works of art should be pure,
in the sense that it is distinguished from all other interests.
One value of the enjoyment of art, in comparison with the
enjoyments that arise from our particular interests and desires,
is that it is an entirely disinterested enjoyment, and that it is
an enjoyment of something universal and necessary in the
human mind, namely, the free play of the imagination; for this
reason it "promotes the urbanity of the higher powers of cognition," in the Henry James phrase of the English translation.
There is therefore both a real analogy between a genuine
aesthetic interest and moral freedom. A serious and unphilis-
tine critic of the arts is a man who always carefully distinguishes his pure aesthetic enjoyment, and his pure aesthetic
estimate of an object, from any sentimental appeal, or charm,
or from utilitarian, or social interests, or from any estimate of
its political or personal desirability, or from its tendency to
edify, or its failure to edify. The question that he always asks
himself is—"Am I sure that the pleasure that I take in careful
attention to this thing is a pleasure solely in the exploration of
the distinguishing and specific qualities of this particular thing,
and therefore one that I may presume to be potentially common to all men, whatever the other differences between them:
common, merely in virtue of the fact that they are all perceiving beings, capable of intense attention to one particular thing,
and possessing imagination; am I sure that my enjoyment now
is an enjoyment in the free exercise of my imagination, which
enables me to see this thing as a whole?" It may then be asked
how the critic can by reflection make sure that he is not deceived in his judgment, self-deceived. First, there are various
negative tests that he can apply in the form of self-examination
or critical reflection. He can ask himself whether his pleasure
is directed towards the existence of this *kind* of thing rather
than towards the satisfaction to be found in his mere careful

attention to this particular specimen, with all its distinctive features of style, form, manner, detail. Where the representative arts are concerned, and particularly the representative visual arts, this entails that aesthetic enjoyment is typically an enjoyment of qualities of form, and of the surprising arrangement of the elements of the work; for the pleasure is not to be associated with the concept under which the thing falls, that is, with the kind of thing it is, or the kind of thing that it represents; it is rather the pleasure arising from the mere process of taking in this particular representation, as a whole and with all its complexities. In aesthetic enjoyment the thing before one is a set of elements so imaginatively arranged as to satisfy the active synthesizing activities of the imagination, which is always involved in attention to objects as wholes. All pure aesthetic enjoyment therefore is an enjoyment of the free play of the mind in arranging a set of given elements as a unity, without classifying them or identifying them. The judgment that something is beautiful is not to be supported, or established, by any test or criterion; it is rather the judgment that anyone who, in face of the object, concentrates solely on his own ordering of his own impressions in the act of close attention, to the exclusion of everything else, will experience pleasure. One may be mistaken in one's judgment that something is beautiful through a lack of critical reflection: but general agreement does not in itself prove that one is right, or general disagreement prove that one is wrong, in calling something beautiful. Nothing whatever can prove this; one can only study the thing again in a proper state of receptiveness and detachment. It is involved in the notion of taste, as a limiting idea which has no empirical content, that there is a sensus communis latent in all men. But this idea is a mere presupposition which cannot be put to any use in the discriminations that we must each make for ourselves. But in making aesthetic discriminations by ourselves, we are separating, as far as we can, empirically ascertainable sources of pleasure, which are not independent of our own contingent psychological needs, from an enjoyment that would be common to all men, if they made the same separation.

This theory does not commit Kant to any of the extreme forms of aestheticism, or to any doctrine of art for art's sake. On the contrary, he is anxious throughout the *Critique of Judgment* to show the morally elevating and refining effects of aesthetic experience and its contribution to the general culture of the mind. Aesthetic enjoyment, being an enjoyment that is detached from the contingent interests of individual men, is a propaedeutic, an introduction to the entertaining of moral ideas. It is also a necessary part of any civilized life in society; it binds men together in an interest that is at once disinterested and humanizing, because it is potentially common to all humanity in spite of all the other differences of interest between men. It is part of the importance of art that, through the possibility of a pure aesthetic estimate, it crosses all the barriers of difference between men at different places and times, and it is the only sure and universal method of communication of feeling based on an interest that can be common to men. Otherwise men are bound together only in the recognition of moral principles and of the regulative principles of scientific inquiry. Apart from the single case of aesthetic enjoyment, feelings and emotions are divisive; and it is only through aesthetic experience that we make the transition from personal feeling to a super-personal and general emotion.

It seems to me that Kant has at least isolated one feature that is common to the various arts, or rather to the nature of our interest in them, and to the importance that we attach to them; he has isolated a ground that we have for grouping the various arts together, in spite of all the differences between them. To consider something and to enjoy it as a work of art, rather than in some other way is, among other things, to detach it, in the process of attention, from all personal and local interests, and from its possible uses. So far an aesthetic interest in human artefacts is not unlike an aesthetic interest in natural objects. But you may doubt whether that which is common to our interest in the different arts, and that therefore composes the concept of art, can be stated without at least some reference to art as always an expression in some medium of the maker's temperament, and of his particular ideals of perfection in that medium. Otherwise we would have provided no place for the concept of style. The work must also be enjoyed as a communication of a mode of feeling characteristic of some men, or group of men, and not solely as a communication of a play of the imagination that is potentially common to all men. The style, the gesture, the movement, the self-betrayal of a particular temperament, and the distinguishing physiognomic properties of a work, are often as moving, and as intimately connected with the peculiar pleasure that a work affords as the purely aesthetic enjoyment. For this reason the original painting has for us, if not for the 18th century connoisseur, a peculiar value, which no faithful copy can have. So far we have therefore only a necessary, but not a sufficient, condition of enjoyment of art.

In isolating the pure aesthetic component, Kant was in effect rejecting the suggestion that the concept of art is a family resemblance concept. There is an essence of art which is present (and is particularly pure and evident) in the art of the light comedian, no less than in the art of the novelist, the pianist, the painter, the sculptor. This is the necessary, preserving element which can be caught by infection, and in that sense imitated by the study of examples, but which cannot be methodically taught or explained by a rule. It is a kind of imaginative rightness in the exact calculation of intervals and patterns, and in the mixing of sameness and diversity, in accordance with some aesthetic idea appropriate to the medium.

But at this point Kant's theory of genius becomes relevant. It is the mark of genius that its products do not show the marks of human contrivance, of the intentional adaptation of means

to ends. In the work of a true genius technique, and the effort
to please, are invisible, and are wholly absorbed. So we have
the impression that the work is not an artefact at all; it seems
entirely natural, in the sense that there is little perceptible
relation between the effect that it makes on the perceiver and
the intentions, purposes and causes that explain its existence.
It is felt to be natural in the sense in which a shell found on a
beach, a jewel found in a mine, or a landscape of mountains
and valleys, are in fact natural. These are all things that can
seem to us, if we abstract from our knowledge of the natural
order, made for our delight, as if they were artefacts. They
are perfectly adapted to our powers of imaginative perception;
but it is only by poetic analogy that we can think of them as
designed to please our imaginations; for we know that we must
think of them as the effect of blind natural causes. So we can
explain the spontaneous enjoyment of beauty in any of its
forms as being a consciousness of this middle ground between
the intuitively natural, which is at the same time known to be
artificial, and the intuitively artificial, which is at the same time
known to be natural. This is a suggested phenomenological
"reduction" of one type of aesthetic emotion, the enjoyment
of beauty, to its source. The source is the narrowing of the
estrangement that we always feel between ourselves as rational
agents and the natural order of which we are also dependent
parts. The gap can be narrowed on both sides. Any great work
of art—say, Othello, or Cézanne's Card Players—is felt to be
a reconciliation with nature, not as an imitation, or shadow,
of it, but as an identification with it, through human achievement. For the effect so far exceeds the means by which it has
been contrived that such works no longer seem to be human
inventions, but rather, like natural objects, they seem to have
an existence independent of conscious design. The strain and
conflict of moral experience, in the will to overcome our given
nature, disappears in aesthetic experience, in which an external object, whether man-made or not, seems to us to be the

realization of an ideal, which we had not previously known that we had in our imagination; so we are for a moment at least, reconciled to things as they are, and the will to act is relaxed.

It cannot be denied that Kant is here presenting, under the guise of a general aesthetic theory, a particular aesthetic ideal of his own period. In Sir Joshua Reynolds' *Discourses,* and in much of the literature of the time, it is suggested that a satisfying work of art should not exhibit the marks of its origin at a particular place and time. The grand style demanded that, for example, the figures in a painting should be generalized, and should not show local idiosyncrasies. So classical drapery might disguise features of dress and bearing that are characteristic of a particular time and place. It is a familiar paradox that this attempt at generality produced a style that is immediately recognizable as a characteristic style of its time. Of Kant's philosophy of aesthetics also one can say that, in his attempt to arrive at the universal statement about the conditions of aesthetic enjoyment, he in fact arrives at canons of taste which exactly reproduce the interests of an eighteenth century connoisseur. The image of beauty, which he suggests in his abstract terms, corresponds to a Gainsborough painting of figures in a landscaped garden, where civilized artifice and controlled wildness meet. The landscape garden of Repton and Capability Brown perfectly illustrates his requirement that symmetry and controlled disorder are universal conditions of aesthetic enjoyment. In a Gainsborough painting (e.g., The Andrewes Family), the natural setting of the park and the house seems to suggest the finality of nature in relation to the human figures, who are visibly at ease in the setting which belongs to them. One sees that they are at home in nature which is itself an artificial disorder. Kant's aesthetics is a metaphysical explanation of the eighteenth-century garden, which is the meeting point of conscious design and of indifferent causality. The rational ideal and the natural order are blended.

When Kant turns to the other necessary and universal feature of men's aesthetic relation to the natural order of which they are a part, the sublime, his general theory again reproduces the taste, and the critical vocabulary, which are characteristic of his time. Reason in its pure theoretical employment tells us that our understanding of nature must always be incomplete. We never arrive at unconditional explanations in our understanding of the natural order. But we are driven to seek such explanations, and so we have metaphysical moods in which we are aware of the limits of our understanding in scientific inquiry and of our powerlessness, by the speculative employment of reason, to understand the natural order as a whole. The equivalent of this demand of reason in our emotional and sensuous experience is a sense of awe before the immensity of the natural order. As a garden is the image of the necessary adaptation of natural phenomenon to our powers of understanding, so a mountain range, or a storm at sea, are the images of the infinite, and of the inexhaustibility of nature, which can be conceived as transcending the categories of the understanding. The revived concept of the sublime is another critical category of Kant's time. The emotional significance of free forms, of an absence of defined outlines, morbidezza in drawing, the conventional excitement of mountains seen through mist, or of the unbounded ocean, are the typical eighteenth century images of men's helplessness before the infinities of nature; robbers in a landscape, minute figures clustered under a stormy sky at the foot of a mountain, were the deeply felt commonplaces of visual art, no less than the landscape portraits which show the transcendental affinity between men and nature. This oscillation between two poles of naturalism is at once caricatured in the art of Kant's century, and yet is asserted by Kant to be a necessary feature of the enjoyment of art at any time.

The pleasure that we take in contemplation in the beautiful is essentially a sense of rest, and of perfect well-being, induced by the adaptation of an object to our powers of observation. The sense of the sublime is a certain restlessness of the mind, a vibration between attraction and repulsion, between humility and the pride of reason, between fear and exaltation. The feeling of the sublime is close to the respect that we feel for rational freedom and the moral law. The sense of transcending our natural condition by the exercise of the reason is the origin of our sensitiveness to the sublime in nature and in art. Even the most primitive people find something sublime in courage, as the overcoming of natural impulse. So to quote, "sublimity does not reside in any of the things in nature, but only in our own mind in so far as we become on occasion conscious of our superiority over nature within (that is, over the limits of our possible perceptions and also of our natural impulses), and thus also over nature outside us." When a man is unable to feel the beauty of something, we accuse him of lack of taste. But we say of a man who remains unaffected in the presence of what we consider sublime that he has no feeling. The difference is that we can presume that every man, however uncultivated, is susceptible of using his understanding; but we cannot have the same confidence that every man is capable of forming ideas of reason, that is, of forming an idea of nature as a whole and of that which transcends our categories. As form is to beauty, so magnitude is to the sublime. The aesthetic judgment of greatness is independent of judgments of beauty; there is an untestable, but universally communicable, impression of greatness, which is an independent category of praise; both natural objects and works of art may suggest to us the limitlessness that we attribute to our reason and to the totalities that it conceives. The feeling of the sublime is closely linked with the metaphysics of morals. It is scarcely conceivable except in association with an attitude resembling the moral, that is, of the sense of the overcoming of nature and of natural limits.

There is therefore a striking symmetry in Kant's account

of the middle ground that lies between the purely normative judgments of morality and the claims to knowledge that we make in the sciences and in the ordinary observation of things. But you will ask, once again, upon what grounds can we be asked to accept his theory of the two types of aesthetic judgment, apart from the symmetry of his own system? Are the terms that he suggests the terms that we actually will employ in critical judgments in works of art and natural beauty?

Consider the range of predicates which we may apply to a drawing, a passage in music, an actor's performance in a scene, a poem, an episode in a ballet, the interior of a church: "stiff," "cold," "clumsy," "awkward," "violent," "crude," "weak," "rough," "gentle," "serene," "subtle," "sensitive," "simple," "coarse," "magnificent," and so on. These are some of the predicates that occur in a critic's vocabulary when he is required to make judgments of quality. They are at once evaluative predicates and perceptual predicates; we may see the stiffness, or coldness, of a movement in a dance, or the crudeness and subtlety of an actor's timing, as definitely as we see the speed of the movement, and hear the interval between one sentence and another. These predicates stand on the middle ground, because there is no learnable rule, or criterion, for their correct application, even though they describe the thing perceived in judgments that are sometimes plainly true and sometimes plainly false. They describe the object with a claim to objectivity, even though the predicates are value-laden and the properties are not measurable properties, which can be methodically detected. Secondly, the violence of colors, and the freedom and roughness of a drawing, are not to be wholly explained as the effects of causes which can be ascertained and the effects therefore achieved by a technique; in so far as they are so explained, and the effects therefore become mechanically reproducible, they cease to be aesthetically interesting. If we can specify completely the means by which the effect is contrived, no place is left for the free play of the imagination. Suppose that we had discovered experimentally, as Burke suggested that we might, why lines of a certain sinuosity are commonly found pleasing. Then the mere fact that we now understood the operation of causes, and the contrivance of the effect, and therefore had a recipe for reproducing the effect indefinitely, would be sufficient to disappoint the aesthetic interest; only a decorative charm, or attractiveness, would remain. The imagination must find its appropriate objects un-intentionally and freely and by surprise. The "must" here is the sign of a conceptual necessity; we will not attribute to the free play of the imagination any pleasure in observation which we can wholly explain by reference to the ascertainable prop-erties of the object. The mystery, or inexplicability, is the con-dition of aesthetic interest. An aesthetic interest has to reveal a relation between any imaginative human observer and the natural order, a relation that cannot be revealed in any other way. Therefore any naturalistic aesthetics has destroyed its subject matter before the inquiry begins. This is no less true of naturalistic aesthetics than of naturalistic ethics. The normative element in aesthetic judgment—"ought this to be enjoyed?"—must be left out of account in a naturalistic aesthetics, which can only relate an experienced pleasure to contingent features of the circumstances in which it was experienced. But then aesthetic enjoyment would be just one pleasure among others and would have no further significance. We know, through this enjoyment, that there is a middle ground which connects our interests as rational beings with our immediate setting within the natural order, adapted to the demands of our im-agination, when it is set free from practical uses.

Henry David Aiken

ON THE CONCEPT

OF A

MORAL PRINCIPLE

THERE HAVE BEEN INNUMERABLE BOOKS in moral philosophy with such titles as "An Enquiry Concerning the Principles of Morals." Some of them to be sure are concerned in part with questions about the meanings of such terms as "right" and "ought," about the logic of moral reasoning, or about the possibility of moral cognition—in short with questions that are assigned nowadays to "meta-ethics" or "analytical ethics." But, as in the case of Hume's *Enquiry,* most, if not all, of them have sought to determine what the substantive principle or principles of morals actually are. Few, however, have asked, in the manner of Kant, how a principle of *morals* is possible; scarcely have asked how, or whether, a *principle* of anything is possible. Indeed, although some attention has been given to the concept of morals and its cognates, there has been little discussion of the concept of principle and almost no systematic effort to provide an independent morphology of principles in the light of which one might hope intelligently to decide whether, or how, there could be principles of morals. It is my belief that some of the confusion and disagreement in moral philosophy is owing to this fact.

In this paper, therefore, I propose to begin by giving some attention to the concept of a principle itself. Then I shall distinguish three main types of principle that are recognized intuitively in everyday talk. Thirdly, I shall say something about the concept of the moral. And then, in conclusion, I shall offer the sketch of a view about the nature and the status of principles in the moral life.

1.   ON THE CONCEPT OF A PRINCIPLE

The etymology of a word is not the same thing as its meaning. Nevertheless a look at its etymology often provides our best initial clue to important facts about the meaning of an expression that have hitherto either escaped notice or else not been brought into proper focus. I have found this to be true of the word "principle." That term, as any respectable dictionary shows, derives from the Latin word *principium* which is generally regarded as a translation of the Greek word *arche,* meaning "beginning," "origin," and "ultimate cause." This fact becomes illuminating in the present connection when we recall that in searching out the beginnings or origins of things, the ancients were usually not engaged in purely scientific inquiries and that, for them, causes, and in particular ultimate causes, were not simply necessary or sufficient conditions for the occurrence of phenomena. For us moderns, or so we pretend, a beginning is just a beginning, an origin only, a point of departure, and cause no more than a constant conjunction. We are often curious about starting points. But we do not suppose that this curiosity entails any particular respect for them, even when the origins in question happen to be our own. We fancy ourselves to be new men, inquiring "objectively" and neutrally about things above the heavens and under the earth, and owing them nothing on that account. Our lives, we fondly imagine, are all our own, or, if not, we are resolutely determined henceforth to make them so. With the ancients it seems to have been otherwise. Lacking our celebrated "historical consciousness," or possibly just because they lacked it, they did not conceive of the past simply as an old curiosity shop. Nor did they regard it as an impediment to be transcended or overcome. Many writers have remarked that the ancients, both Greek and Hebrew, tended to look back nostalgically to the past as if to a golden age which, physically irrevocable, ought yet to be recalled and, through memory, to give meaning, substance, and direction to their lives. For these ancients, in short, preoccupation with origins was a moral or religious concern with the authoritative sources—I was about to say "principles"—of their being, a way of establishing their own identity and legitimacy as persons or as a race. Or, to put the point in slightly different terms, the study of origins was at the same time viewed as an act of piety toward that *arche* or principle which provided the authorization for what they were, what they were to be, and, in short, for what we call their "way of life." From this perspective, what was "in the beginning" provides a continuing purpose, or principle, that justifies and gives significance to one's life, perhaps even to existence itself. Accordingly, one whose origins and hence principles remain unknown is one whose status is uncertain, and one without origins, or principles, is one who lacks an established place in the sun, one who is without a settled way of life, in whom therefore it would perhaps be hazardous to repose a trust. In a word, any question about an *arche* or principle when the *arche* is one's own, is obviously a matter of immense personal importance. It provides a basis of one's identity as a person, and, in the process, establishes a regimen for one's conduct of life along with the burden of responsibilities such a regimen imposes.

These casual etymological remarks are not, I believe, without use when we consider the current meaning of the term "principle." They help us to see, for example, what there may be in common, however obliquely, between the sun, viewed as a principle of light, the embryo, viewed (as the Catholic Church views it) as a principle not just of human life but also of human personality, certain highly general propositions such as are characteristically referred to in speaking of "the principles of physics," "the principles of logic," or "the principles of the sonata form," certain commonly unverbalized strategies which we refer to as "the principles of chess," or the "principles of naval warfare," and finally, but by no means least, those personal rules or precepts to which we refer in speaking of "our religious principles," "his legal principles," or "my moral principles."

For present purposes, however, it will be convenient henceforth to restrict our discussion to certain modes of utterance. Now it is essential to observe that one cannot tell whether a given utterance is a principle merely by scrutinizing its grammatical or logical form. Nor, as a general rule, is any light shed on the question whether an utterance is a principle by noticing its specific conceptual content. Perhaps it is true that the presence of the word "God," in its religious employment, suffices to invest certain utterances in which it occurs with the status of principles. Or, better, it disposes us, in many circumstances, to regard utterances in which it occurs as principles. For the most part, however, one must look beyond the particular terms occurring within a proposition in order to determine whether it is functioning as a principle.

But the very locution "functioning as a principle" provided a clue to an understanding of the use, or role, of the concept of a principle. And in fact the concept of a principle may be defined as a "functional concept." By this I mean, negatively, that in speaking of anything, for our selves and for our own part, as a principle we are not describing any of its physical characteristics, as we do in speaking of it as "heavy" or "round;" nor are we specifying any feature or aspect of its characteristic behavior as a thing or object or phenomenon, as we do, for example, in talking about its bodily processes or movements; nor, finally, are we referring directly to the reactions that organisms of a certain sort make to certain objects, as we do when we say that an object is desired by or pleasing to some individual or group. More positively, I mean that the concept of a principle, in its primary active employment, serves essentially to assign to that to which it is applied a privileged role or status in a certain sphere of activity. Again, anything acknowledged to be a principle is thereby invested with a certain authority over a scheme of thought or action. And when a speaker seriously applies the word "principle," in its primary and active sense, he thereby serves notice that he for his part acknowledges its authority over his own behavior in relevant situations. In still another way a principle resembles a promise in that the affirmation of it, as such, automatically involves the person who makes the affirmation in certain obligations within the sphere covered by the principle in question. In short, if something is, and is seriously asserted to be, a principle, then some particular person or class of persons is in some way bound to subordinate or to be ready to subordinate his or its actions to it. And if it is denied that the thing in question is a principle, then this is tantamount to a denial that some person or group of persons owes it any allegiance.

In order to obviate certain misconceptions, however, it is essential to remark in passing that it is true generally of functional concepts, including the concept of a principle, that they may be used in an inactive as well as in an active sense. Thus, just as I can speak of Smith's promise without thereby committing myself to the performance of any action, so I can refer to another's principles without being in any way beholden to them. But such an inactive use of the term "principle" is logically dependent upon another, active use, independently of which the inactive use could not be understood.

2.

Principles may be conveniently divided into three main classes which I shall refer to respectively (a) as "disciplinary" principles, (b) as strategic principles, and (c) as preceptive principles.

(a) As the term suggests, disciplinary principles specify the definitive policies, procedures, and (if any) offices of a discipline. I employ the term "discipline," here, in a wide sense; by it I mean any form of activity, for example, a science, an art, a social practice, or, most broadly, an institution, that is concerned with the realization of certain impersonal, public ends and/or with certain characteristics, more or less settled, ways of doing things. A discipline is logically independent of the interests, attitudes, or sensibilities of any individual, private person or persons as such, including those who may happen on occasion to serve as their functionaries or officers. Like all things, human disciplines are subject to change, but even when their changes are effected by the identifiable decisions or actions of individual persons, that fact itself has nothing formally to do with their status as disciplinary changes. More clearly, changes acquire disciplinary status only when they enter into the constitution of the discipline as modifying principles.

Disciplinary principles are characteristically designated by such impersonal locutions as "the principles of physics," "the principles of common law," or "the principles of justice." And they are thereby sharply distinguished from personal principles which are normally exemplified by such formulas as "Newton's physical principles," "my legal principles," or "our principles of justice." Logically, disciplinary principles are constitutive of the disciplines which they govern. As such, they must be understood by anyone who properly claims to understand the discipline in question. They also must be taught by anyone who offers to introduce novices into a discipline; and they must be learned by anyone who is entitled to claim a minimal competence in the discipline. And more generally, acceptance of them as authoritative guides to belief and action is not a matter of choice for anyone who, as such, represents the discipline.

Now in situations where disciplinary principles become a subject of dispute among disciplinarians, where they are no longer regularly taught to or learned by ordinary apprentices to the discipline, the discipline so far automatically breaks down, thereby losing its status and distinctness as a discipline. This does not necessarily mean that every thesis or hypothesis, every particular rule or activity, within the discipline thereby fails; it means only that it is now cut loose from the discipline and must henceforth make it on its own or else find its way into some other discipline. In modern science, I am told, a process of democratization is now setting in, so that traditional lines between disciplines are becoming blurred, questions of method are not so readily settled in advance or without regard to specific results. It is conceivable that we could find ourselves in a situation in which we are no longer able to speak confidently of *the* science of geology, or even of *the* science of logic, but only so to say, of science and its problems. As a limiting case one can perhaps imagine circumstances in which, except programmatically and philosophically, one could no longer speak of the principles of science or even of the principles of scientific method or inquiry. In that case, if one still did so, then despite the fact that no determinate consensus any longer existed and no authoritative commitments any longer held in common by would-be "competent" persons, the role of such claims would now be mainly to keep open the possibility of reestablishing or reconstituting the discipline and hopefully to minimize the significance of disagreements and disaffections until the discipline could be reconstituted on another basis.

In order to avoid false issues, it must also be borne in mind

that most disciplines are in fact continually threatened with
break-downs of one sort or another, through spreading incom-
petence, slovenly teaching, unexemplary teachers and indifferent apprentices, "young turks" within the discipline who want
immediately to reform it, or growing indifference or hostility
to the discipline within the society of which it is a part. In our
thinking about institutional realities, we are well advised to
think in terms of degree. Our conceptions of the arts and
sciences, and indeed of all practices and activities, to some extent idealize the actual performances of the persons involved.
Correspondingly, every actual principle is subject to a certain
vagueness both in itself and in relation to other principles. No
principle is adhered to in an absolutely undeviating or routine
way; nor is its place within a discipline perfectly well-ordered
and well-defined. There are always, as it turns out, unantici-
pated hierarchical questions of precedence that cannot be resolved with certainty by appealing to other ordering principles.
Built into most principles are explicit or implicit "unless
clauses" that cannot be authoritatively filled out by routine
appeals to pre-existing principles for the making of exceptions.
And, in sum, there is a certain unavoidable or even desirable
roughness about the edges of all disciplines which is necessarily
mirrored in their defining principles.

   In a full treatment of disciplinary principles, it would be
illuminating, or indispensable, to consider them systematically
in relation to situations of perpetual crisis, revolution, or radical social change. In a slightly different way, it would be useful to studies of the sort in which we are here engaged to
develop a sort of dialectical phenomenology of the liberal and
the conservative, the loyalist and the revolutionary, the bureau-
crat and the enthusiast, and then systematically to relate it to
the theory of principles. Here it must suffice to remark that
within every historical discipline, one finds, in relation to its
principles, inescapable ambivalences that are reflected in the
tensions which develop within it between principled passivists

who quietly and simply observe the rule and activists who follow it, as we say, on principle, between those who make an issue of principle of each problem of choice that arises, and those who try to resolve it by *ad hoc* measures which have the effect of reducing the principles of a discipline to the status of ceremonials, loyalty to which reduces them to a matter of ceremonial observance. In this sphere what is wanted, I fear, is a new Hegel who combines the characteristic historical and dialectical sensitivities of a Hegel with the modern analytical philosopher's preoccupation with prevailing uses of expressions and the existentialist's acute awareness of what it is to have one's being at the end of time.

(b)   About strategic principles we may be more brief. If disciplinary principles set the terms of competence within a discipline, strategic principles state conditions of mastery, of success, or, more negatively, of avoiding failure, within the discipline. If learning the disciplinary principles is a condition of bare competence, learning, and being able to apply, strategic principles is, generally, a condition of doing well. Strategic principles are obviously characteristic of games where problems of winning or not losing are at stake. And in speaking of the principles, as distinct from the rules, of a game, we normally have in view strategic, not disciplinary principles. Conversely, minimal competence in a discipline is never definable in terms of a knowledge of strategic principles. Likewise, introduction to strategic principles is normally deferred until the constitution of the discipline has been set out. And when well established strategies acquire, as they sometimes do, so definitive a role that competence in a discipline begins to be conceived in terms of *them,* their whole significance undergoes a sea change, and it becomes more important to the initiate that they be followed than that he should really try to win. For him, so to say, "defeat with honor" is, so far as the discipline is concerned, now more to be prized than the achievement of victory. But true strategic principles, adopted and sustained with a view to their role in securing success or in avoiding failure, always remain *advisory* principles. And violation of them is always justified, relatively to the ends which they serve, when a sounder strategy, in the circumstances, presents itself.

Strategic principles may be conveniently classified as "institutional" or "non-institutional." By "institutional strategic principles," here I mean simply those non-personal authoritative strategies, adherence to which is normally required for achieving success (or avoiding failure) within the sphere of an institution or a discipline. It is institutional strategic principles, of course, that we usually have in mind, for example, in speaking of the principles of a game or a sport or of the principles of, say, naval warfare, although such principles are by no means restricted to games, sports, and military disciplines. But now we come in sight of another characteristic difference between strategic and disciplinary principles. For even institutional strategic principles, unlike disciplinary principles, may be private and personal as well as public and non-personal. But this is not true of disciplinary principles. For example, any chess player may adopt special strategies of his own which, when their efficacy has been established through practice, acquire the status of principles which the player departs from only reluctantly and when there is a compelling reason. Such principles remain genuine institutional principles since their ends are conceived in terms of success or the avoidance of failure within a discipline. But they are, nonetheless, personal principles in the sense that they are adopted by particular individuals for whom alone, by hypothesis, they have any authority as principles. Institutional strategical principles may also be private in the sense that their virtue as strategies, depends in part upon their remaining unknown to anyone but the individual strategist himself. In short, although institutional, they are not common property, not part of the public lore of the discipline in question, and indeed, cannot, as such, become so.

But there are also, plainly, non-institutional strategic principles adherence to which is (or is deemed to be) required for achieving some success not achievable within the framework of a discipline. Each of us, for example, has strategies for achieving certain preferred results, for doing well, or avoiding failure, in some sphere of action which we entertain for our own pleasure or interest. In time these may become authoritative guides to judgment and action which henceforth we violate only with reluctance and for good reason. Non-institutional strategic principles, it should be added, may be held in common by a number of persons for the purpose of realizing some end which they happen to share. But for all that they remain personal principles, since their being principles at all depends solely upon the fact that the persons involved adopt them in order to bring off some results which they happen jointly to seek.

(c)   In discussing strategic principles, the notion of a preceptive principle has already been introduced informally. It is time, however, to say something more explicitly about them. As the phrase suggests, preceptive principles are first-personal precepts adopted by particular persons and dependent for their authority and status as principles entirely upon such persons' loyalty to them. Preceptive principles are characteristically identified by locutions essentially involving the use either of possessive pronouns such as "my," "our," "his," and "their," or else of proper names (or their equivalents). Qualifying adjectives are also frequently introduced into expressions serving to specify particular preceptive principles. These in turn serve either to indicate certain conventional forms or spheres of activity within which the principles are to be applied or else they serve to specify certain characteristic problems to which the principle in question is addressed. Thus, for example, I may speak of Justice Holmes' legal principles, in which case I am referring to certain preceptive principles adopted by Holmes himself for guidance in reaching his legal decisions; here the qualifying adjective "legal" refers to the sphere of professional activity in which Holmes worked and in which he took such an intense personal interest. But I may also speak, say, of Spinoza's metaphysical principles, in which case, it is at least arguable that the qualifying adjective "metaphysical" serves not so much to specify a well-established and clearly marked sphere of public activity—in short a public discipline—but rather a vague area of interest in which certain characteristic problems arise.

Now, all preceptive principles are, as it were, for the time being. That is to say, their status as principles, and hence their authority, is contingent entirely upon the conscientious submission of the persons who adopt them. In saying this, however, I do not mean to suggest that, as principles, preceptive principles are any less weighty or any less serious than disciplinary principles. I mean only that they exist as principles only in the adoption and through the continuing reaffirmation of those who avow them. A few further remarks may help to obviate other misconceptions. In speaking of preceptive principles as principles which do not exist save in so far as they are personally adopted and avowed, I do not in the least wish to convey the impression that whereas disciplinary principles are splendidly objective, impartial, disinterested, or impersonal, personal precepts are on the contrary subjective, partial, interested, and invidious. There is no reason why my principles may not be arrived at circumspectly, objectively, or why they should not enjoin me to be impartial, disinterested, and impersonal. For want of time, I shall say no more about this matter here, but the point, although obvious enough, is crucial, particularly for the understanding of moral precepts.

Many other things would have to be said both about principles in general and about our three types of principle in a full-dress analysis of the concept of a principle. I am aware that I have not provided an account of the concept of authority in this paper, although the concept of authority is essentially involved in the notion of a principle. There are also further interesting similarities and differences among our three types of principle upon which I lack time for general comment, although in passing something will be said about a few of them when we come to the problems of determining the status of principles in the moral life.

3.

Something, also far too schematic, must now be said about the concept of morals itself.

Let us first distinguish between inactive and active uses of the term "moral" and its cognates. The word "morality," for example, is sometimes employed, quite inactively, in mentioning the prevailing social code of a social group, including on occasion the group to which the speaker himself happens to belong. In such a case one may conscientiously reject "morality" or else be harshly critical of it without falling into paradox or contradiction. This, I take it, is what is meant by the phrase "positive morality," which, as such, has nothing necessarily to do with what the speaker as a conscientious moral being ought, or believes he ought, to do. In this inactive sense, one may speak, in a purely descriptive, sociological or anthropological vein, of the morality of the people of East Lansing, the morality of the Trobriand Islanders, or, perhaps, the morality of the Age of Reason.[1]

I shall not pause to remark upon the corresponding in-

---

1. In this inactive sense, questions about the unity and diversity of morals, such as Professor Morris Ginsberg concerns himself with, may be approached in a purely neutral way. Nor is it clear what relevance they have for moral philosophy. From the point of view of the moral agent, at any rate, nothing essential turns on the answer to be given to the question: Are all moral codes essentially similar? For it could be true that there is, underlying the apparent diversity of moral codes, a pervasive unity; yet one might feel that such a moral unity, as it stands, is wrong and ought to be opposed. Correspondingly, it could be that there is a fundamental diversity of moral codes, yet one could argue that this diversity ought to be removed, and that all men ought to live together under one universal moral principle.

active uses of the cognate terms, "moral," "morals," "moralize," "moralistic," and the rest. Moral philosophy, for example, may or may not be a good thing, and philosophers often concern themselves at least with its more analytical parts in no more engaged a spirit than they concern themselves with faculty meetings or the grading of examinations. But one may use the word "morality" itself in an active way in speaking, not of the principles or rules of a social group, but rather of those principles of conduct which, as one believes, are right principles, the principles, that is, by which one ought to live. Here the term "morality" is employed in the sense sometimes associated with the phrase "critical morality," which has been introduced, partly for this purpose, in active contradistinction to positive morality. In this sense it would indeed be paradoxical to ask whether one ought to act in accordance with the demands of morality. And were anyone to ask it, the question would suggest, in its paradoxical way, that he was for some reason, and at least for the time being, wholly disengaged from the moral life. He would be *showing,* so to say, that for him morality is "dead" in a way analogous to that in which theologians show something about themselves when they assert, no less paradoxically, that God is dead.

But let me now introduce a distinction which cuts clean across the one just made between the active and the inactive uses of the word "morality" and its cognates. Here I shall confine my remarks to senses of the adjective "moral," rather than to the nouns "morality" and "morals," to which the distinctions I have in mind do not so obviously apply. There is, to begin with, a very wide sense of the term "moral" which we sometimes employ in speaking, for example, of a moral certainty. Here the word "moral" seems roughly equivalent to the word "practical." Again, philosophers sometimes speak of philosophy as a form of activity as having a moral, rather than a purely speculative or theoretical or scientific purpose. And here too, I take it, they mean primarily to suggest that philosophy is concerned, in the last analysis at least, with the conduct of life, with questions concerning how one is to live rather than with neutral questions about matters of logic or of fact. In this sense, I suppose, a moral principle would be simply any practical principle some one felt prepared to live by or, better, any principle by which, in conscience, some one felt ought to guide one's actions.

It is worth remarking at this point that most, or all, of the so-called "ethical terms," about whose meanings moral philosophers have been debating throughout the present century, share with the word "moral" this capacity for application throughout the whole range of human conduct. And it is just for this reason, in large part, that moral philosophy, or ethics, so far as it concerns itself primarily with the so-called ethical terms, is impossible to distinguish from axiology, the general theory of valuation, or the analysis and critique of practical judgment and reasoning.

There is also a well established, but narrower sense of the term "moral" which many philosophers have in view, in their discussions of moral principles and principles of morals. Here, I contend, the term is used, on its inactive side, to refer simply to the domain of personal and perhaps (although this by no means comes to the same thing) human relations. Moral principles, from this point of view, are principles which are treated as authoritative guides in solving, or resolving, problems concerning our conduct toward persons. The pressing question plainly is whether problems about personal relations are problems that can plausibly be viewed as occurring essentially only within the framework of a discipline of morals or, on the contrary, whether the very notion of a covering discipline is inapplicable to the relations that hold among men as persons.

In discussions of personal relations, the term "moral" is also employed actively, and in explicit opposition to the term "immoral." In this use it presents a contrast which is closely parallel to the familiar oppositions between the terms "right" and "wrong" and—most importantly for our purposes—"ought" and "ought not." Thus to say that an act is immoral is, in effect, to say that it is wrong and/or that it ought not to be performed. Likewise to say that an action is moral is, depending upon the context, to say either that it is not wrong to perform it or else, more positively, that it is a right action, the thing to do, or that it ought to be performed.[2] Now, in the active sense here in view, a moral principle is nothing more than a principle of right action, a principle for determining what one ought to do in situations in which one faces a problem of personal relations. In this active sense, furthermore, to say that a principle is a moral principle—or, if such there be, a principle of morals—is to imply that one ought to appeal to it in deciding both how one ought to judge, and how one ought to act, in particular cases. In a word, a moral principle is, quite explicitly, a principle of conduct, a principle *to be* followed, in one's practice, and not just in one's thought, in one's dealings with other persons.

4.

We come at last, to the matters with which this paper is most centrally, if a bit tardily, concerned. For we have now to consider the nature and status of principles in the moral life.

Let us begin by asking, in a somewhat dialectical mood, what happens, what to expect, when people speak actively of principles of morals. Our answer, I believe, is already prepared for us. In the first place, we are disposed to think that for them, at least, "morals" refers mysteriously to a kind of discipline,

---

2. Obviously, a number of refinements might be introduced at this stage, but the interest of this paper does not turn upon them, so I shall say no more about them here.

like physics or the common law. Let us call it, for the sake of discussion, the discipline of personal relations. Here, one is led to fancy the moral agent as a kind of functionary, an office holder, one who has certain established responsibilities and rights. Further, one is led to think of professors and students of morals—the former offering, or being prepared to offer, courses entitled "Morals I" or "Introduction to Morals," and the latter taking such courses, along with pass examinations in them.

But now, following this model, let us consider a prospective student of morals a bit more closely. For him as an individual there is always the question whether to go into morals, or if he is already in, to go on with his apprenticeship. Perhaps he has failed the pass examination, the first time around, and is now somewhat discouraged. He realizes that he has assumed certain duties as an apprentice, but these are onerous. And so he asks himself, as he is entitled by the terms of the model to do, "Why go on with this? The duties are heavy and I really don't see what the point of it all is. Or, rather, I see what the point of being an agent of morality is, in view of my instruction, but I don't see the point of *my* becoming an agent of morality. So I think I will quit. Now I realize that I will probably feel a sense of shame, at first, as one always does when he does something a bit outre, something that goes against the established order. I realize, in short, that I won't have measured up to the requirements of the discipline, and am now so to say being flushed out. I will become an outsider. It isn't pleasant, I can see, to be an outsider, and to be made to feel that one isn't qualified, that one doesn't really belong. But then so it is and I've got to do it."

It would be easy to go in this vein, but I spare you. Surely, anyone who conceives of the moral life in such terms as these has not penetrated its essence—if it has an essence; nor is he equipped to cope with the most crucial and agonizing of moral problems. In a word, he is not yet morally adult. Indeed, I was about to say—perhaps using the word "moral" in its full, active sense—he is as yet scarcely a moral agent at all.

But now, as analytical philosophers you will doubtless require something more than this by way of criticism—although I think that what has been said already suffices to show that the phrase "the principles of morals" has a very hollow ring. Let me then make a few somewhat more technical observations. If there *are* principles of morals, as there are of physics or of arithmetic, then it should be possible, without too much difficulty, to cite some of them, and further to cite them in such a way that no one who has a (supposed) moral competence can seriously ask, "But ought I, at least now, to do as that principle requires?" Or, to put the point in another way, one ought to be able to provide paradigm cases, and not just exemplary instances, of a principle of morals. But this is what I am unable to provide and what others who have attempted to provide it have not managed to do. On each occasion when a putative paradigm is offered, I find it to be, at best, merely exemplary. Indeed, in the circumstances I, like Gide's principled immoralist, am virtually impelled to reject it, if only to prove a point.

One further observation: If there were paradigmatic principles of morals, it may be supposed that they would hold only, as we say, *ceterus paribus*. But among the other things to which the principle—say, for example, the principle that all promises ought to be kept—may be unequal are certain first-personal moral precepts which, in the circumstances, require one to violate the principle of morals. The point is simply this: A principle of morals, or even a code of such principles, does not suffice to make a discipline of morality, so long as one may be bound, in conscience, to violate such principles in order to do what one's personal precepts require. The moral thing to do is, tautologically, what one ought to do. But what one ought to do is beyond the power of any discipline whatever to settle beyond peradventure. One may *always* decide, upon reflection, that one ought to do, or not to do, *this,* though the heavens fall.

If there were a full-fledged, definitive discipline, or institution of morals, then it would still remain to the particular person to decide for himself whether or not to participate in the discipline and hence to become one of its functionaries. Surely, this is precisely *not* the way any of us confronts the moral life. I do not decide, in general, to enter a discipline of moral relations with other persons. Rather do I find myself already deeply, infinitely, problematically, involved with them, and in ways that do not stay put. My moral insight, such as it is, changes, develops, is transformed in an instant by a consideration, a preception, a possibility I never before entertained.

What is the alternative? The suggestion has been explicitly made by John Dewey in *Human Nature and Conduct,* that there are principles of morals, but that they are to be viewed by the critical moralist as strategic rather than as disciplinary principles. This way of viewing morality also has a certain dialectical interest, to which I can do no justice here. For one thing it disposes us to think of moral actions—Dewey likes to call them "lines of action"—as well tried strategies for winning moral victories. Now the moral agent becomes a gamesman who hopes henceforth to win at the game of morals or else to do well in his job as a moral functionary. But suppose one simply tires of winning moral victories or is no longer really interested in one's moral successes. Suppose one, at last, wants merely to be let alone and to forget the vanity of moral "achievements." To such a person the talk of strategies is merely fatiguing and their authority is nil.

Beyond this, most of the criticisms that can be raised against the view of principles of morals as disciplinary principles can also be raised against the view of them as strategic principles. In sum, such a conception of moral principles does violence to what may be called the phenomenology of the moral life, including, above all, the sense of personal responsibility and guilt, the need to make amends, the sense, above all, that one's principles are, for oneself, whatever they may be or seem to be for others, categorically binding.

Let me hide no longer behind my dialectical mask. In my view, theories of the moral life that ask us to conceive of morality as a discipline or as a set of strategies for winning moral victories or avoiding saddening moral failures are not only mistaken but, to the extent that they are taken seriously, deplorable. Not only is the moral life *not* like a game of chess or a career in the sciences, it is, for my part, morally wrong to so view it. Moral principles are, and are to be regarded as, preceptive principles. For only when so regarded is it possible to think of them, as Kant correctly insisted, as categorical imperatives which the moral agent himself follows because for him it is inescapably the right thing to do. To be sure, disciplinary principles also present themselves as categorical to the unmitigated functionary. The station with its duties leave the functionary no genuine alternatives. That, indeed, is, if I may say so, just the trouble with him. But the moral agent, as such, is not and cannot be one who is nothing but a station and its duties. He is also one who, if I may borrow a leaf from Kierkegaard, *may* find, when and if he takes thought, that he ought to suspend any and all stations and their duties in order to kiss a leper.

But now, at the last moment, must the moral agent not ask himself: "Could I will the maxim of this act to be a universal law?" Must he not ask himself whether, if he were a leper he would care to be kissed? Must he not universalize in any other sense than sense itself requires? My answer is "No." Any one *may* do all of these things, according to his lights. But no so-called discipline of morals, no principles of morals, no perspective called "the moral point of view" can oblige him to do so. The moral life is the prerogative of free men who, in Kant's paradoxical phrase, "give themselves the law." But of course a law which one gives oneself is no law at all. What one is left with is merely one's own awareness of commitment, of guilt, of the need to make amends, and endlessly to try again. To convert all of this into a discipline or into a strategy is to violate it in its heart of hearts, just as to convert the love of God into the observance of a law is to fall into idolatry. In a way, indeed, to talk of the principle or principles of morals is itself already to fall into moral idolatry. And in the long run this may well turn out to be one of the profoundest of moral faults.

John Wild

IS THERE AN

EXISTENTIAL

A PRIORI?

I BELIEVE THAT A SENSE of being in possession of an un-
expressed and latent knowledge is not restricted to professional
philosophers but is more widespread among reflective minds
than is commonly supposed. Certainly the notion of *a priori*
concepts and principles only vaguely known by us but nevertheless conditioning the unstable opinions which guide our
everyday activities has been a major theme of Western philosophy since its beginnings. Thus in his doctrine of reminiscence
Plato held that our knowledge of geometrical truths concerning straight lines, circles, and triangles, never observed in sense
experience, and of moral norms, like justice, never achieved
by any particular actions, must come from a prior source,
though he did not use the term *a priori*. Since it cannot be
accounted for by information derived from the senses, such
insight must be due to glimmerings of a prior knowledge
gained in a prior state when the soul had access to the timeless
ideas before it drank of the waters of Lethe and entered into
the confused and ever shifting realm of becoming.

Analogous conceptions are found in Augustine and the
Augustinian tradition, in Descartes and Leibnitz, and many

other philosophers. But it is the Kantian formulation which has left the deepest mark on the tradition of modern philosophy in the West. According to Kant, there is no world of perception, for without concepts, percepts are blind. He speaks of sense data as a chaotic manifold. And without a transcendental synthesizing principle, holding these data together by the forms of intuition and the categories, no organized, objective experience would be possible. These ordering principles are, therefore, *a priori* in the sense that, even though they may never be clearly focused, they are presupposed by even the most rudimentary experience, and are, therefore, universally and necessarily operative in all men.

If we ask what these various conceptions of *a priori* knowledge have in common, I believe that we shall find three features at least which can be distinguished. First, in all of its many versions, it is due to intelligible structures to which all men have access. They therefore give rise to principles of knowledge which are not limited to any special situation, or circumstance, but which hold for all men necessarily and universally. This is true not only of the Platonic view and its derivatives, but of the Kantian version as well.

In the second place, these *a priori* principles are either temporarily and/or logically prior to the variable and particular facts of experience, and condition them in the sense of giving them a basic order and meaning. Thus on the Platonic view, it is only by virtue of the *a priori* forms that the individual, flowing objects of experience become partially intelligible as plants, animals, beds, houses, and so forth. And on the Kantian view, it is only by virtue of the forms of intuition and the categories, that the manifold of sense, as he calls it, is ordered into an intelligible world of objects. In laying down these underlying patterns of experience, the *a priori* principles also condition intelligible discourse and science, which are necessarily concerned with empirical objects. Thus common experience, discourse, and science all presuppose these principles which are *a priori,* or prior to them in a temporal and/or a logical sense.

Finally, in the third place, these principles, though constantly at work, are nevertheless largely hidden from our waking consciousness. Thus the geometrical truths that lie ready in the mind of the slave boy in the Meno, have to be elicited and made explicit by the skillful questioning of Socrates, and the Kantian transcendental unity of apperception and the categories are brought into the light only by an elaborate transcendental deduction. Of course we are not completely ignorant of them. According to Plato, without some faint awareness of the pure forms, we would be unable to recognize and name the confused imitations that appear before us, and according to Kant, without the transcendental unity of apperception and its forms, no orderly objective phenomena would be possible. But on all these views, our *a priori* knowledge is originally very dim, and faint, and implicit, and lies on the fringes of our waking consciousness.

Now as I see it, these three traits of *a priori* knowledge, as universal and necessary, as presupposed by concrete experience, ordinary discourse, and science, and as hidden, are recognized, with certain variations, in all the important versions that have so far appeared. As I see it, no version lacking any one of these could properly be called *a priori.* So, these traits will appear in the empirical theory that I shall present. However, before turning to this new theory, we need to examine the traditional tendency to discount the world of sense which goes back to the Greeks, and which disqualifies this world (if it is a world at all) from being *a priori* in the three essential senses just mentioned. First of all, Plato compared the objects of sense to the fleeting shadows in his Cave. Being in constant flux, and not remaining on hand long enough even to be mentioned without slipping away, it seemed clear to him that these particular shifting data have only a minimum of stability and structure derived from an alien source. Hence of themselves they fail to provide us with any adequate foundation for any universal knowledge, common to all men. Following the British empiricists, Kant refers to this "world" in similarly disparaging terms as a mere "manifold of sense." Such discrete particulars may give us material content. However, they cannot provide us with the formal patterns which are clearly required not only for *a priori* knowledge in an eminent sense, but even for the most rudimentary awareness. They are, therefore, unable to qualify as the ground for an *a priori* knowledge that is universal.

Second, on the assumption that these units of perception are discrete particulars, there is no reason for supposing that there is any necessary connection between them. After one has happened, any other might occur. Certain ones may occur before others in time. But to be sure of this, we must wait for them to happen. Such knowledge is *a posteriori,* even though the sequence may repeat itself indefinitely. In such a scheme there is no way in which any one impression, or set of impressions, may condition, or be presupposed by another set. Hence such discrete sense data cannot meet the second criterion of *a priori* knowledge—conditioning a whole range of phenomena which cannot occur without them.

In the third place, an impression may become faint. But as long as it exists at all, it is definite and distinct. As such, it must either be or not be. With this picture in mind, it is hard to see how any one of these, such as a sweet taste, can be semi-present in a condition that is vague or half-concealed. It must either be there or not there. The notion of fringes, and of a field of perception were not developed until the time of William James, Husserl, and the Gestalt psychologists of the nineteen twenties. But in the traditional conception of experience, shared by both rationalists and empiricists, there is no total background, no fringes in which objects may be first dimly felt, and then slowly clarified by a new concentration of attention. Hence sense and feeling, as traditionally conceived, fail to meet the third criterion of the *a priori*—semi-consciousness and concealment.

This discounting of the world of perception has led to that radical opposition between the empirical and the rational which is such a marked characteristic of traditional thought. On the one hand, we have the elements of sensation, like blue color, middle-C sound, and pain, which are discrete and unrelated; on the other, universal concepts which subsume these elements, and then subsume each other in an ordered hierarchy, thus relating them into a meaningful system. Hence the perennial issues between rationalism and empiricism, each singling out one of these factors for special emphasis and subordinating the other. This radical separation has brought forth the famous story of the two worlds, that of sense where opinion alone (*doxa*) is possible, and the intelligible world of reason (*nous*), or now language, which is the *a priori* condition for the former.

Let me now briefly mention four definite conclusions which follow from this intellectualistic, or in more contemporary terms, *linguistic* version of the *a priori*. First of all there can be no pre-conceptual or pre-linguistic knowledge. What William James called a dumb knowing by direct acquaintance is impossible. What he called "the world of sense" is merely a senseless manifold. No *a priori* structures can be found in experience. They are found only after they have been imposed by a conceptual or a linguistic system.

In the second place, rational concepts or conscious linguistic formulations are prior to perception which involves implicit judgments of some kind, in so far as it becomes aware of definite objects. The whole notion of preconceptual, or preconscious, semi-conscious awareness is ruled out. Third, the basic phenomenological effort to find what Husserl called "pre-predicative patterns" is a naive mistake, for how can we try to describe any pattern of lived experience without a conceptual or linguistic frame already in mind. No pure description is even possible. Finally, fourth, the *a priori* patterns that order the whole of the human world are, therefore, not to be found in experience. They are to be found rather in the prior patterns of logic and/or language.

Until the coming of what James called *radical empiricism,* and what now goes by the name of phenomenology, this conception of *a priori* knowledge, with many minor variations, has dominated the history of Western thought. It is very much alive at the present time in the form of what we may call a *linguistic idealism* which identifies the *a priori* with the ordering patterns of language. I shall now turn to a critical examination of this conception, beginning with the arguments for discounting the world of sense, and ending with the four conclusions we have just noted. In the course of this examination, I shall be suggesting and, so far as the time permits, defending a new, and what we may call a radically empirical conception of *a priori* knowledge which is now emerging from the disciplined investigations of phenomenology. Many anticipations of this new conception are to be found in James' great work *The Principles of Psychology* (1890), to which I shall often refer.

In this work, James attacked the Kantian doctrine of empirical data as an unrelated "manifold," and adopted the opposed view that the relational parts of experience are perceived in the same way, and just as originally is its substantive parts (I, pp. 243–48). This became a cardinal principle of his radical empiricism which he defended against the widespread disparagement of the world of sense by the empirical and Kantian schools of his time. The strongest part of this defence was his success in revealing certain relational patterns which remain constant as the particular contents vary, and thus "always" hold as necessary conditions for such experience. One of these is the continuity, or stream-like character, of the field of consciousness which he analyzed with great care (*Principles,* I, pp. 237–71).

Today this would be called an example of phenomenological description and analysis. So I think it may be worth a brief quotation and comment. Let us then take one of his examples, the hearing of a thunder clap. We have two words for thunder and silence. So it is easy for us to fall into the empiricist view, which is really a covert form of rationalism, and to think of these as two distinct impressions which follow each other, first silence, then thunder. But as James points out, following Brentano, this is an oversimplied distortion of what we actually feel. "Our feeling of the same objective thunder . . . is quite different from what it would be were the thunder a continuation of previous thunder" (*Psychology,* I, pp. 240–41), for this feeling bears within it something of the past. As James puts it: "into the awareness of the thunder itself the awareness of the previous silence creeps and continues; for what we hear when the thunder crashes is not thunder *pure,* but thunder-breaking-upon-silence-and-contrasting-with-it."

Hence he refers to our experience as "a stream of thought" whose substantive parts are constantly related by feelings of transition. Here is a relational pattern which holds for particular experiences, and which seems to be prior to linguistic and conceptual formulations. For surely the young child hears thunder and is frightened before he knows the words. In fact, if James and the phenomenologists are right, this feeling of transition in the specious present is opposed to what the artificial separations of language would lead us to expect. But this, and other patterns of our pre-conceptual experience, can be described and expressed by a disciplined use of language, as I believe this example shows. Any experience will take place in the continuous flow of a specious present. This would seem to be an *a priori* condition for any lived experience. There are many other preconceptual patterns of this kind which have now been at least partially brought into the light.

For example, there is the oriented lived space, which is prior to the perceptual experiences of our waking life and conditions them *a priori*. There is also the active living body, not as it is objectively observed, but as it is felt and lived from the inside. At the end of his career, in his *Essays in Radical Empiricism,* James speaks of this lived body as follows (p. 170). "The world experienced (otherwise called the 'field of consciousness') comes *at all* times with our body as its center, center of *vision,* center of *action,* center of *interest.* Where the body is is 'here'; when the body acts is 'now'; what the body touches is 'this'; all other things are 'there', and 'then' and 'that'. These words of emphasized position imply a systemmatization of things with reference to a focus of action and interest which lies in the body; . . ." Then skipping a few lines: "the body is the storm center, the origin of coordinates, the constant place of stress in all that experience-train. Everything circles around it and is *felt* from its point of view."

James then proceeds to identify this active, living body with the self. "The word 'I' then", he says, "is primarily a noun of position, like 'this' and 'here' ". But while this 'I' is the source of subjectivity, it is not a transcendental ego separated from the world of meanings that it organizes around itself. It is *in* this world, and in this oriented space of which it is the active center, so that the very same activities which are lived and felt from the inside can, in part at least, be observed and measured from the outside. Later on Husserl also, near the end of his career, became deeply interested in this living body (cf. *Krisis* pp. 108–10), and noted its close connection (*leibliche Ichlichkeit*) with what we call the self. Still later, Merleau-Ponty has developed these ideas in his phenomenology of perception (the *phenomenal body* or *le corps vécu*). That I must live and operate in a field of which my lived body is the institutional center would seem to be another *a priori* condition for lived experience.

If the world of direct perception, the world of sense, as James called it, can no longer be discounted as a mere sequence of discrete impressions; if it possesses stable field structures which remain invariant as particular content changes, then the notion of an empirical *a priori* knowledge becomes possible. We do not have to get outside the world, and outside of our bodies to gain a transcendental position from which we can ask how this is possible. Perhaps we cannot gain such a position.

If there is an empirical *a priori,* we must gain access to it in another way. As we remain in the world with our bodies, we must catch these patterns of existence, with the aid of memory, imagination, and feeling, in the very act, as we live them through. These are not *a priori* structures of meaning only, pure possibilities that condition actual experience. They are rather patterns of existence, *relational facts,* as we may call them, which condition the particular facts of our human histories. Of course these structural facts are not *absolutely* necessary, since human existence is contingent. But they are bound up with this existence so that we can say: as long as man factually exists, these structures, being in the world, the lived body and its basic patterns of behavior, lived space, the continuous flow of lived time, for example, will always be found.

It is true that these patterns are originally only vaguely perceived, and that even after words have been found for them, the meanings of these words usually fade off into the dimness of the obvious, which is never clearly seen but always taken for granted. I am not sure, however, that this vagueness should be accepted as evidence against their *a priori* character, for, in my own experience, at least, clarity and certainty vary inversely. As long as I follow my lived perception and leave it vague, I am, like Augustine, sure about time, that it is going on, and that I am involved in it. As soon as I look at it, however, in terms of a clear-cut theory that spells it out, I begin to doubt, not time itself, which is *a priori,* but the way in which it is clearly explained. Of course, we need clarification. But we also need to retain the original perceptual certainty, which should belong to what is truly *a priori*.

If William James and his successors, the radical empiricists and phenomenologists are not mistaken, these patterns like being-in-the-world, the lived body, space and time, will be found universally and necessarily wherever man is found. Furthermore, they lie at the ground of all the varying particular experiences which make up human history. Hence our knowledge of them, so far as we possess it, meets the first two general criteria for the *a priori*. But how about the third? If there are necessary factual patterns of this kind, why should they be so extensively neglected and ignored? Why do they tend to remain hidden and half-concealed in the obvious?

Here I must introduce the notion of another perceptual structure, first clearly focused by James, which had a basic influence on Husserl, Gestalt psychology, and the whole future development of phenomenology down to the present day. This is his notion of "fringe", or what he often referred to as "the field conception of consciousness". This conception can be summarized as follows. Our attention is ordinarily focused on specific objects of practical or theoretical interest. It is now recognized, however, that such definite figures never appear except on a vague field, or background, of fringes, fading off to a distant horizon. Language and conceptual thinking, in general, enable us to sharpen this focusing of attention by inventing separate words for supposedly separate objects. But at the same time, they lead us to neglect the background and the grounding patterns on which these figures appear. This tendency is strengthened by the fact that the boundaries of these fields are imprecise, and their patterns only dimly and vaguely grasped at the level of perception, whereas the major emphasis in sophisticated linguistic usage is on clarity and precision. Hence the classical empiricists almost totally missed this field conception.

It is true that we have words in common usage for time, the world, and the self. But for the most part, the original perceptual meanings of these terms have slipped into the obscurity of the obvious, a form of the semi-conscious. Hence when asked, we are apt to confuse the world with all the things in the world, time with the various things that occur in time, and the self, with an identical thing, or subject, separated from all other things and perhaps outside the world altogether. But then we forget the empirical *a priori,* that without a world horizon there can be no things in the world, and that without time itself, there can be no succession of things in time.

This now offers us a way of accounting for the partial concealment of this empirical *a priori.* With our basic tendency to focus on specific objects, the world horizon and the subordinate fields of space, time, and self are shoved off into the fringes where they lapse into a dormant, semi-conscious or "obvious" condition, from which they can be rescued only by the arduous techniques of radical empiricism or phenomenology. It will also serve to explain a remark of James on his whole procedure for which he has sometimes been taken to task by his more logically and intellectualistically oriented critics. "It is", he says, "the re-instatement of the vague to its proper place in our mental life which I am so anxious to press on the attention" (*Principles of Psychology,* I, p. 254). The evidence we have tried to suggest in this brief time indicates that the traditional arguments for the discounting of perceptual knowledge are unsound. There is a world of perception marked by stable structures which meet our three criteria for the *a priori.* They hold universally and necessarily for all men. They condition particular experiences, and are presupposed by ordinary language and science. Finally, they are normally hidden in the fringes of the objects of our attention, and require disciplined, phenomenological, methods to be clearly focused.

Now let us turn to those four intellectualist conclusions

concerning the *a priori* which have been derived from this disparagement of perception. I believe that these conclusions are also unsound. According to the first, we can gain no knowledge of stable, *a priori* structures in perceptual experience. But in the light of recent findings in phenomenology, this assertion is now open to serious question.

Pre-conceptual experience is not a chaotic manifold of discrete impressions, but a vast world horizon including many sub-worlds and regions. I believe that phenomenology has now shown that such basic characteristics of linguistic consciousness as intentionality, meaning, temporality, retention, protention, understanding in a broad sense of this term, and purposive striving are all present at the level of perception where objects are presented to us in their original bodily presence. This world is pervaded by ambiguity, for perception is dominated by its object, and the fringes are always vague. But similarities and differences are recognized. Order and meaning are present in a confused way, and are ready to be linguistically clarified, fixed, and communicated. Hence reason does not appear on the scene as a completely alien intruder into an empirical chaos where order must be created *ex nihilo*. The way for clarification, completion of meaning, and communication has already been prepared.

Furthermore, this pre-conceptual world is not subjective, for in it things are presented in their actual bodily presence. So there is no need for any dualism of the sensible versus the intelligible as disorder versus order, or as the subjective and relative as opposed to that which exists in itself.

Perception already begins, in its limited way, to reveal things as they really are, and language goes on with the task. Reason, as it has been called, needs perception for a grasp of being in its corporeal presence and a dim apprehension of its basic structures like figure and ground, space, time, and the living body. Perception needs reason and language for clarification, the completion and fixation of partial, floating meanings, and finally for communication.

But how about the second intellectualist trait of the traditional conception of the *a priori*. Are clear-cut concepts and linguistic formulations prior to perception? I have shown you, I think, that this assertion also is now open to serious question. Language has arisen in the *Lebenswelt*. Indeed though it presupposes other patterns, like world and the living body, it is a necessary structure, for wherever man and the world are found, language of some kind, though not any one language nor system of conceptual categories is also found. To speak and to think are ways of being in the world, and perception is another. They represent two different levels of *a priori* intentionality, each lacking something possessed by the other, and needing support. There is no need for two worlds. The one in which we live is rich, and far-ranging, and vast enough.

But if each supplies something lacking in the other, how, more exactly, are language and perception related? Which one is prior to the other? Are we then in a position to turn the tables on the traditional intellectualistic view? Can we at last defend the notion of an empirical *a priori* which is prior not only to particular experiences but also to language and conceptual discourse? As my whole argument has been suggesting, I believe that we can. There is evidence which tends to show that instead of experience being originally conditioned by language and its structures, it is the other way round. Language and reason are incomplete, and are constantly conditioned and limited by indeterminate structures of experience and perception. I have already indicated the general nature of this evidence. But let me now try to break it down into four lines of argument which I shall now suggest, in each case with a brief comment.

Let me begin with another example taken from James (*Psychology,* I, pp. 221–22). This is concerned with references to unverbalized perception which are expressed by articles, pronouns, and by the grammatical "subject" of any meaningful sentence or discourse. Such discourse takes place in a total situation which is already known directly, to some degree, by feeling and perception. This knowledge by *direct acquaintance,* as James calls it, is presupposed. Thus as he says (p. 222), "the minimum of grammatical subject, of objective presence, . . . the mere beginning of knowledge must be named by the word that says the least (conceptually). Such a word is the interjection, as lo! there! see! voila! or the article or demonstrative pronoun introducing the sentence as *The, it, that.*" If this reference to the unverbalized is lost, we fail to see what the discourse is about and it sinks away towards mere verbalism. Does this not indicate that language rests on a prior kind of knowledge which it presupposes? Does it not always occur in a situation that is somehow already understood? Is it not surrounded by fringes of meaning that are never fully expressed but have to be read, as we say, between the lines? In speaking of a life situation, can everything ever be said? Is there not always something left over which, to use current phrases, is beyond all words, or even inexpressible? But in saying this, do we not show that we are aware of it in a prelinguistic way.

A second line of investigation is concerned with *a priori* structures of the world of perception to which we have referred, such as lived space, lived time, and the living human body. Is it possible to clarify these structures by language and reason alone without constantly referring back to the perspectives of perception according to the methods of phenomenology? Is it not true that language presupposes these structures? Is not speaking (thinking) a way of being in the world? Would language be possible without a world that is already present, and without things and persons already there in the world to talk about? Does it not require an active, living body that is able to move in the fields of time and space? In order to suggest a justification for an affirmative answer to these questions, I shall mention only those recent studies of perceptual space by Merleau-Ponty and others which show its close relation to bodily motions and its pre-conceptual origin.

Furthermore, if there is no pre-conceptual world that is presupposed by intelligible discourse, how can we explain the well-known, Kantian dangers which arise when language and thinking lose real contact with the world of sense that is prior to them? Any concept, or theory, or speculative system which fails to take account of this prior world and its structures, and passes beyond the limits they impose cannot be taken seriously as a real possibility. It may be an empty conjoining of words with no real meaning. So the Kantian work of criticism needs to be constantly resumed and sharpened, though in a different and wider context.

But even if there is a primordial world of perception which is always present on the fringes of our discourse, and presupposed by it, we may still raise questions as to how it is known. We may still argue that while this world and its structures are there, it cannot be known and accepted until it is expressed in propositions and, therefore, subjected to the *a priori* patterns of language. An *"a priori"* that is *completely* unknown certainly cannot qualify for what has been meant by this term. Is there any evidence to show that this requirement can be met, that there is a primordial awareness of the whole perceptual world and its structures? I believe that there is such evidence. During his symbolic calculations the calculator may, of course, and should doubt his projected proof and its special evidence. But should he entertain any serious existential doubt, as we may call it, concerning the whole world in which it is taking place and his existence in it, the demonstrative action would be interrupted. For this world background is presupposed.

James referred to this primordial acceptance of the world by the term *belief.* Husserl in his *Erfahrung und Urteil* used the term *Urdoxa* (in conscious opposition to the Platonic tradition). We have used the word *feeling* but it seems also to involve an element of trust in the world as we engage ourselves in it, and a hope to be sustained by it. Back of the special noetic attitudes involved in the use of language: doubt, uncertainty, inquiry, probability, certainty and so forth, there seems to be a more pri-mordial belief in the real world as a whole which is pre-linguistic in origin, but which is still maintained with the coming of language, and is presupposed by its special manifestations. Thus just as there is an all-encompassing world horizon with its stable patterns that are prior to language and discourse, so there seems to be a prior kind of belief in this world, an *Urdoxa,* which is prior to more special forms of knowledge. Hence seriously to doubt the whole world which includes the doubter, or any of its basic patterns, is something more than a logical contradiction. As psychiatrists would say the human sense of reality is involved. It is not merely discourse but its existential foundations that are also affected. We might call this, for want of a better term, as we shall soon point out, an existential contradiction.

Now, how about the third trait of the intellectualist or linguistic view of the *a priori?* Does it stand in the way of our describing a perceptual pattern as we live it through? As some linguistic idealists now think, does it make phenomenological description impossible? Our pre-verbal, pre-thematic awareness of the world is vague and unanalyzed. But in this very sentence, we have verbalized it, and we have constantly stressed the need for conceptualizing and clarifying, if it is to be fully understood. This raises a basic question. Can the pre-linguistic patterns of which we have been speaking be linguistically expressed without fundamental alteration? If not, this pre-verbal *a priori* can never be clearly expressed, and the whole conception I have been trying to express in words will be basically undermined. Is there any example of pre-linguistic meaning, at first vaguely grasped which then is clearly expressed in words without serious distortion? I cannot argue the issues in detail. But I shall offer an example taken again from James' *Psychology,* Volume I, page 253. He speaks here of the intention to say something before we have said it.

We are apt to dismiss this transitional state as one of complete ignorance, but this is far from the truth. We can reject the wrong words and feel the rightness of others. But this feeling is still in an indefinite and unformed state. As James says: "Linger and the words and things come into the mind; the anticipatory intention, the divination is there no more. But as the words that replace it arrive, it welcomes them successively and calls them right if they agree with it, rejects them and calls them wrong if they do not. It has, therefore, a nature of its own of the most positive sort, and yet what can we say about it without using words that belong to the later mental facts that replace it? The intention-to-say-so-and-so is the only name it can receive".

Here is a meaning, an eidetic pattern, as Husserl would say, known directly by direct acquaintance. We must first feel what we want to say. In order to say anything clear and communicable about this feeling, we must use words. But this does not mean that *it* is originally verbal. It is a distinct condition that is definitely pre-verbal.

Furthermore it is a noetic condition, which knows something before it is said. Otherwise it could not select the right phrases and reject the wrong. When a right step is taken, it reverberates and answers back. So, by following these answers, we may be led to the right expression. Of course a change has occurred—the meaning has become analyzed, clarified, and communicated. But it is the same meaning, the same pattern that is expressed.

The status of what I am calling the empirical *a priori* is similar. It is first known by what James called "the way of direct acquaintance" (I, p. 221) or the dumb way of acquaintance. This is irreplacable and presupposed by language. It must first be lived through to be verbally expressed. But its

meaning *can* be clarified and communicated, for if we are
ready to listen, it will respond to our attempts at verbal formulation. In this way the *a priori* patterns of our lived experience
can verbally be revealed.

Finally, let us look at the fourth trait of the traditional
view of the *a priori*. According to this view, the basic patterns
of existence are not to be found empirically by examining the
fields of perception. They are to be found rather only by a
transcendental deduction from experience to its logical conditions, or by a study of language. This doctrine also is open
to serious questions on phenomenological grounds.

These patterns of perception do not come from another
intelligible realm. They are not imposed on the world of sense
by a separate worldless mind or language—they are *found* in
the pre-thematic world of perception, *ingrained* in it. Hence
we do not arrive at a clear formulation of them by any purely
logical deduction which uses perception only as a starting
point, but only by a careful dwelling on the phenomena in the
dialectic process of reverberation we have just described. Here
logos and language do not act alone but only together with the
lived phenomena to find *their* logos, inherent in them.

Furthermore, when these *a priori* conditions of human
existence are doubted, together with the vague acceptance of
them which James called *belief,* something more than logical
contradiction is included, as we have noted. Here also the empirical *a priori* differs from traditional versions. Such doubt is
concerned with the *a priori* conditions not only of reason and
discourse but of human life. Such statements as *I am asleep*
being made by a waking man, *I am not sure that I exist, there
is no truth,* belong to this order. Such propositions are self-
contradictory in the sense that they contradict *a priori* conditions without which their actual assertion would be impossible.
For want of a better name we have called them *existential
contradictions,* for when seriously meant, they manifest a dis-
integration of existence. In this way, what we are calling the

empirical *a priori* differs from traditional versions, for violations, or denials, of these lead only to logical contradictions which leave our existence intact.

Ever since the time of Plato, philosophers in the West have been digging down under the statements of our ordinary and scientific discourse in the attempt to discover its ultimate roots. What are the ultimate presuppositions which underlie our speaking and thinking? What are the ultimate patterns which condition the life of our human existence? If such patterns could be brought into the light, it would not only clarify what we may call the human condition—the things that all men possess in common—it might also strengthen the possibility of real communication between different groups and peoples, and of laying sound foundations for the human sciences.

I believe that these purposes are of great importance, and I am glad that this digging has been going on. I am sure that it will continue to be a major pre-occupation in the further development of philosophy. But, as I have tried to show, until very recently, this whole enterprise has perhaps been proceeding in the wrong direction. Instead of looking for the *a priori* in the world of sense and feeling, it has looked for a conceptual or linguistic *a priori* in a universe of discourse artificially isolated from existence. Hence the aims of the enterprise have been frustrated. Instead of looking towards existence to find out how men *are,* these diggers have focused their attention on divergent ideas of what men *ought to be.* Instead of examining the existential conditions which all men share in common, they have concerned themselves rather with the different languages and conceptual systems which divide men from one another. Instead of trying to find real patterns in the actual human world, they have postulated different ideal patterns that have been pre-fabricated and imposed on experience, rather than found in it with the aid of perception and feeling. So the whole enterprise has failed, and instead of becoming more luminous, the notion of man has become ever darker and more obvious.

In these remarks I have tried to suggest a new notion of the *a priori,* an existential *a priori,* which is now beginning to emerge from the investigations of phenomenology. This *a priori* is found in existence with the aid of perception and feeling, rather than imposed upon it from the outside by a sovereign reason. Hence it has begun to shed some light on the existential conditions which men share in common rather than on the linguistic schemes that divide them. It has been easy to find tribes and peoples whose everyday speech differs markedly from any list of supposedly basic categories. But it is not easy to find any tribe or people, no matter how primitive or advanced, which is not at least vaguely familiar with the world in which it lives, with the oriented space in which it moves, the time *through which* it lives and faces death, and the living body which anchors it in the world. Can any individual anywhere be found who, for example, will not grasp the meaning of a blow on the face?

This then is the empirical *a priori* which I have been trying to suggest to you. Instead of abandoning the whole notion of the *a priori,* as they have tended to do in the past, I believe, therefore, that empirically oriented philosophers should work out further and defend the empirical *a priori* to which their own empiricism should lead them, that is, if, like that of James, it is an empiricism that is really radical.

Aron Gurwitsch

THE HUSSERLIAN CONCEPTION
OF THE INTENTIONALITY
OF CONSCIOUSNESS

Husserl's definition of consciousness in terms of its intentionality marks a revolutionary innovation in the history of modern philosophy. It solves a problem which, on the grounds of the traditional modern conception of consciousness, proved hopelessly enigmatic, or to say the least, it prepares the problem in question for a promising theoretical treatment. Hence it appears opportune to consider Husserl's theory of intentionality historically, though, to be sure, this theory must ultimately be judged on its own merits. Its validity can only depend upon its satisfactorily accounting for the fundamental structure of consciousness. Still, to present it historically does bring forward its full significance in the most striking fashion.

In order to formulate the problem which Husserl's intentionality theory attempts to solve, we shall first sketch the general conception of consciousness which dominated modern philosophical thought since its beginning with Descartes. According to that general conception, which may be accurately

termed the theory of Ideas,[1] the only objects to which the mind
or the conscious subject has direct and immediate access are
its own mental states. Consciousness is conceived as a self-
contained and closed domain, a domain of interiority completely severed from what may be called the domain of externality which, in turn, comprises whatever does not belong to
the former domain. It is this separation between the domain
of interiority and that of externality, between the *res cogitans*
and the *res extensa,* which defines the *Cartesian Dualism.* In
the domain of interiority, events and occurrences of diverse
nature take place; this domain comprises multifarious contents and data. Notwithstanding the differences among them,
all these contents, happenings, events, and occurrences are on
a par insofar as they pertain to the domain of interiority. Hence
their belonging to this domain qualifies them as subjective and
defines their status as psychological facts. Among these subjective psychological occurrences are some which have or
claim objective reference, that is to say which refer or claim
to refer to entities other than mental states, occurrences
through which a stone, a house, a triangle, another human
being, and the like present themselves. It is the class of such
subjective occurrences as distinguished by the mentioned reference or the referential claim, that have traditionally been
denoted as *Ideas.* It cannot be stressed too emphatically that
in this view Ideas, notwithstanding their distinctive feature,
are and remain subjective occurrences, psychological events,
mental states, to commerce with which the mind or consciousness is forever confined, among which alone, so to speak, the
conscious subject moves. At this point, the principle underlying the theory of Ideas can be expressed in the form in which
it has repeatedly been stated in the course of modern philos-

1. In order to avoid confusion with the specific sense in which Hume uses the
term of "idea", we are writing "Idea" (with "I") to denote the general sense which
that term has with Descartes and Locke.

ophy: *the only direct and immediate objects of our knowledge are our own Ideas.*[2]

At once the question arises as to how Ideas as subjective occurrences in consciousness can mediate or establish, in any way whatever, contact with, or access to, trans-subjective or non-subjective entities. How can psychological events ever have or acquire significance beyond being subjective mental states? The question can be expressed in a different and more general form. We have or claim to have knowledge of objects which pertain to the external world, be it knowledge in the sense of common experience of perceptual objects in the everyday world, be it, in the specific modern sense, scientific knowledge concerning the objects of the external world in their "true" and "real" condition. The Cartesian term *res extensa* refers to objects as understood in the latter sense. In either case, our knowledge is arrived at through subjective processes which are its vehicle and its only one. Again we must ask: how can subjective processes which take place within the domain of interiority have, or even claim, reference to extramental, trans-subjective entities and events which, by definition, fall outside the domain of interiority and, for that reason, are called objective? Not only must the claim under discussion be justified, but its very possibility must, prior to such justification, be accounted for. It must be made intelligible that

---

2. The first explicitly to formulate this principle was, as far as I can see, Antoine Arnauld: "Il est très vrai que ce sont nos idées que nous voyons immédiatement et qui sont l'objet immédiat de notre pensée." (quoted by E. Bréhier, *Histoire de la philosophie*, vol. II, 5th ed., Paris, Press Universitaires de France, 1947–50, p. 219). Further formulations of the principle are found in Locke, *Essay on Human Understanding*, Book IV, ch. I, §1: "Since the mind, in all its thoughts and reasonings, has no other immediate object but its own ideas, which it alone does or can contemplate; it is evident, that our knowledge is only conversant about them."; Hume, *Treatise of Human Nature* (ed. L. A. Selby-Bigge, Oxford, at the Clarendon Press, 1958), p. 67: ". . . nothing is ever really present with the mind but its perceptions or impressions and ideas . . ."; Kant, *Kritik der reinen Vernunft* A 98–9: "Unsere Vorstellungen mögen entspringen, woher sie wollen, . . . so gehören sie doch als Modifikationen des Gemüts zum inneren Sinn, und als solche sind all unsere Erkenntnisse zuletzt doch der formalen Bedingung des inneren Sinnes, nämlich der Zeit unterworfen . . ."

Ideas and other subjective occurrences and processes can, as
they do, pretend to objective reference and cognitive significance.

Our intention is not to pursue the discussion of this central
problem of modern epistemology arising on the basis of the
Cartesian Dualism in general terms. Rather we propose to concentrate on a special aspect of that problem which seems to us
to be its fundamental aspect. Ideas, subjective processes, and
occurrences of every kind and description are not only as they
are experienced, but their being or existence is completely defined and totally exhausted by their being experienced. An Idea
appears, endures for a certain length of time, and disappears.
Once it has disappeared, it never can reappear again. To be
sure, another Idea, highly similar to it, even perfectly like it,
may emerge in its place. Still, the mere fact that one Idea has
made its appearance prior to the other shows that we are dealing with two Ideas, separated from one another by a shorter
or longer interval of time, that is to say we are dealing with
different Ideas, whatever relation of similarity or likeness may
obtain between them. In short, no Idea or other mental state
can ever recur in strict identity. On the other hand, the objects
to which we have access by means of Ideas present themselves
as identical over and against the multiple occasions of our
dealing with them. The books we now see on the shelves are
the same as those we saw yesterday, on numerous previous
occasions, and which we expect to see again whenever we
enter our room. Normally and as a rule, we do not reflect upon
the identity of the objects with which we concern ourselves,
we do not disengage their identity nor make it explicit. Rather
we simply and implicitly accept the objects as identical; we
take their identity for granted and avail ourselves of it in proceeding upon its unformulated acceptance, though we are at
every moment free explicitly to formulate and to explicate
that identity by an appropriate reflection. At any event, the following question arises: *How can the implicit or explicit con-*

sciousness of identical objects or of the identity of objects ever be conveyed by Ideas, if the latter, *as just mentioned, merely succeed one another, without any of them ever recurring?* If, as Locke maintains, "the mind knows not things immediately, but only by the intervention of the ideas it has of them," [3] how, in the absence of identical Ideas, can the mind come to know the things as identical?

It is the historical merit of Hume to have formulated the problem under discussion in the most radical and sharpest terms. Differing from Locke, but in agreement with Berkeley, Hume does not admit the distinction between objects and perceptions. Unlike Locke, he does not presuppose the independent existence of objects as defined by the "primary qualities" in contradiction to Ideas (in the Lockian sense) by means of which the mind enters into contact with those objects. According to Hume, "those very sensations, which enter by the eye or ear, are . . . the true objects . . . there is only a single existence, which I shall call indifferently *object* or *perception* . . . understanding by both of them what any common man means by a hat, or shoe, or stone, or any other impression, conveyed to him by his senses." [4] Impressions are involved in the aforementioned incessant temporal flux. They are "internal and perishing existences",[5] which is to say that once an impression has disappeared it never recurs again. Now we can formulate our problem.

We believe ourselves to be in the presence of identical objects if, while staying in our room, we alternately open and close our eyes, or if, after having left our room, we return to it, whereas the perceptions or impressions, which are given

3. Locke, *Essay on Human Understanding*, Book IV, Chap. IV §3.
4. Hume, *Treatise of Human Nature, op. cit.*, p. 202.
5. *Ibid.*, p. 194; cf. also p. 253: "The mind is a kind of theatre; where several perceptions successively make their appearance; pass, re-pass, glide away, and mingle in an infinite variety of postures and situations . . . The comparison of the theatre must not mislead us. They are the successive perceptions only, that constitute the mind . . ."

before and after either interruption, differ from one another, it being "a false opinion that any of our objects, or perceptions, are identically the same after an interruption".[6] To account for the origin of the belief in the identity of objects, Hume resorts to the high degree of similarity between successive perceptions.[7] Because of that similarity, the mind, in passing from one perception to the next, finds itself in the same, or nearly the same, disposition as that in which it is when, without an interruption or other variation, it surveys an object or an enduring perception.[8] The belief in the identity of the object is due to the imagination. Hume goes as far as to consider that belief is a fiction which the imagination produces in making us oblivious of the interruptions of the perceptions. Consequently, the imagination can work and the belief in question can be entertained as long, but *only* as long, as our obliviousness lasts. As soon as we remember those interruptions and become aware of the perceptions as being multiple and diverse, the belief under discussion is shaken and we become perplexed.

What is crucial in Hume's account is not so much the ascription of the belief in the identity of the object to the imagination, nor his characterization of this belief as a fiction, nor even, finally, the fact of the operation of the imagination being impeded. Rather, we submit, the central thing is the way in which the problem is set up. According to Hume, "the notion of the identity of resembling perceptions, and the interruption of their appearance" are two opposite and contradictory principles.[9] Their conflict cannot be resolved unless one principle is "sacrificed" to the other.

As just mentioned, the operation of the imagination consists in making us oblivious of the interruptedness of our multi-

---

6. *Ibid.,* p. 209.
7. For the following cf. *Ibid.,* pp. 201 ff.
8. For the sake of simplicity we disregard the complicating problems besetting the experience of a perception as enduring in time.
9. Hume, *Treatise of Human Nature, op. cit.,* pp. 206 f.

ple perceptions or, as Hume expresses it himself, "we disguise, as much as possible, the interruption, or rather remove it entirely." [10] To repeat it again, the point at issue is not that the "disguise", "removal", and "sacrifice" is unfeasible, but rather that the very formulation of the problem proves to be at variance with the phenomenal state of affairs, as can be shown by the simple example previously mentioned.

When, while seated in our room, we close and open our eyes, we are free to ascertain that the books we are perceiving now are taken by us to be identically the same as those which we perceived a moment ago (before closing our eyes), a long time ago (before we had left our room), and which we expect to perceive as identically the same whenever, while staying in our room, we look in the appropriate direction. The identity of the object perceived and the multiplicity of the acts of perceiving the object—acts located at different moments of time and, hence, separated from each other by temporal intervals— are far from being principles contradictory to, and exclusive of, one another, as Hume's theory has them. On the contrary, in becoming explicitly aware of the identity of the object we by the same token also become explicitly aware of the multiplicity and diversity of the acts of perception. *The explicit disclosure of the identity of the object perceived is not only accompanied by, but even requires explicit awareness of the acts of perception as multiple,* since the identity of the object perceived cannot be ascertained and rendered explicit except in opposition, therefore with reference, to the multiple occasions of perceiving it as identical.

It is not in an arbitrary way nor by mere chance that Hume was led to formulate his problem in these terms. The logic of his system motivated and even necessitated that formulation. Therefore, the critique derived from confronting his theory with the phenomenal state of affairs does not concern a mere

10. *Ibid.,* p. 199.

detail of his theory, but its very foundation. Beyond this it
concerns the theory of Ideas itself which Hume has presented
in its most consistently developed and elaborated form. In
fact, if Ideas (in the sense of Locke) or perceptions (in
Hume's parlance) are the only objects which are directly and
immediately given, and if these Ideas or perceptions are involved in an incessant temporal flux and variation, then it is
utterly unintelligible that the consciousness of identical items
and, in the case of explicitation, the consciousness of the
identity of those items can arise. The analysis of Hume's theory brings to the fore the fundamental phenomenon which
must have its place in every theory of consciousness, namely
the fact that through multiple acts the same object can, and
does, present itself and that its identity can be disclosed and
rendered explicit.

The importance of the phenomenon in question was clearly
seen by William James who formulated it under the heading
of "the principle of constancy in the mind's meanings" as follows: "The same matters can be thought of in successive portions of the mental stream, and some of these portions can
know that they mean the same matters which the previous portions meant." [11] However, it is not sufficient simply to establish
that principle, even while recognizing it as "the very keel and
backbone of our thinking", as "the most important of all the
features of our mental structure". James could content himself
with proceeding in this way, because, writing as a psychologist,
he deliberately abstained from entering into any problem concerning the possibility of knowledge. From the point of view of
psychology as a positive science knowledge can, and even
must, be admitted and taken for granted as an "ultimate relation" between the "mind knowing" and "the thing known",
two "irreducible" elements between which a "thoroughgoing

---

11. W. James, *The Principles of Psychology,* (Dover Publications, Inc., 1950, vol.
I), pp. 459 f.

dualism" and a "pre-established harmony" obtain.[12] If, however, the problem of the possibility of knowledge is raised, as it must be within a philosophical context and even within that of a radicalized psychology, the "principle of the constancy in the mind's meanings" cannot be stated alone, but must be inserted into a general theory of consciousness. In view of the failure of Hume's endeavors, such an insertion cannot mean reducing the consciousness of identity to something else nor accounting for it in terms of something else. On the contrary, the fact that the same object presents itself as identical through multiple acts must be made the cornerstone of the theory of consciousness, which is to say that the theory must start from it and throughout remain centered upon it. Finally, the fact in question cannot be simply stated and postulated, as James may be said to have done. Rather it must be disengaged and disclosed through a descriptive analysis of acts of consciousness.

With these remarks we have arrived at the threshold of Husserl's theory of intentionality or, what comes down to the same thing, his phenomenology. Within the limits of the present paper, there can be no question of presenting the theory of intentionality in its entirety, not to speak of all its ramifications.[13] We shall not only limit ourselves in the main to perceptual consciousness, but even within these limits we must further confine ourselves to emphasizing a certain aspect which, to be sure, seems to us to have paramount importance for both the theory of perceptual consciousness and the theory of intentionality in general.

Let us return to our example. Seated in our room and alternately opening and closing our eyes, we see on the shelf

---

12. *Ibid.*, vol. I, pp. 216 ff.
13. The notion of intentionality plays an important role in all of Husserl's writings. Q. Lauer in his *Phénoménologie de Husserl* (Paris, Presses Universitaires de France, 1955) has studied the development of the theory of intentionality through four works which had appeared in Husserl's lifetime.

a book which we perceive to be the same entity presenting itself on different occasions, i.e., through multiple acts of perception, and we may render its identity explicit. At this point a higher degree of preciseness is called for. As it stands on the shelf, the book turns its back to us; we see it from its back; furthermore, we perceive it at eye level; it occupies a central position in our field of vision. If we turn our head, the book is relegated from its central to a rather lateral position; or it might be placed on a higher or lower shelf. By motions on our part, namely by placing ourselves at different points of observation in our room, the spatial orientation in which we perceive the book is changed. Finally, the book may lie on the table so that we see it from some other side than its back. We may see and touch it at the same time; we may open it, move it, lift it so as to perceive it as heavy or light; we may act upon it in many other ways. Throughout we take the book with which we are dealing as one and the same thing presenting itself in various manners.

As the analysis of this example shows, every perceivable thing appears as identical through various and diverse acts of perception, such that as the perceptions succeed one another, the selfsame thing presents itself under varying aspects, from different sides, in various orientations. Insofar as through any given perception the object appears under a certain aspect rather than a different one, every particular perception is essentially one-sided or, to express it in Husserl's terms, through every particular act of perception the thing perceived presents itself by way of one-sided adumbration.[14] Thus we ascertain an opposition between the perceived thing as an identical unity and the multiple perceptions which differ from one another on

14. Husserl, *Ideen zu einer reinen Phänomenologie und phänomenologischen Philosophie* I (henceforth referred to as *Ideen*) pp. 73 ff. (the page numbers refer to the original edition 1913; the edition in the *Husserliana* vol. III, 1950, indicates on the margin the pagination of the original edition). Cf. also *Cartesian Meditations* (translated by D. Cairns, The Hague, M. Nijhoff, 1960) §17.

account of the identical perceived thing presenting itself under various aspects and in varying orientations. More precisely, it is an opposition between the identical thing as susceptible of appearing in multiple adumbrational presentations, on the one hand, and, on the other hand, those adumbrational presentations themselves, all differing from one another, in which the thing appears through successive perceptions.

The opposition just brought out must be distinguished from that which we emphasized in our critical analysis of Hume's theory. Suppose the thing perceived to be immobile and suppose further that we remain at our point of observation or, after having been absent for some time, return to it so as to resume our observing the thing from the same standpoint. We experience multiple perceptions, e.g., a new perception at every reopening of our eyes. Through all of these perceptions, not only does the same thing present itself, but it also appears under the same aspect, from the same side, in the same orientation, and so on. Here the opposition is between the thing as appearing in a particular one-sided adumbrational presentation, on the one hand, and, on the other hand, the multiple perceptions through which the thing thus appears, the perceptions being, of course, psychological events which take place at a certain moment of time and differ from one another at least as to the point of time in which each of them occurs. In the case of the opposition mentioned before, that between the perceived thing as such and the multiple perceptions through which the thing appears in varying manners of adumbrational presentation, the perceptions involved are also psychological events differing from one another as to their places in phenomenal time. In addition to that difference as to temporal location, there is in this former case a further difference which concerns what may provisionally be called the "content" of the perceptions, insofar as the thing in question is perceived through them from different sides and in varying perspectives. But in the case of the opposition now under consideration the perceptions agree in "content", have the same "content" and only differ with regard to their places in phenomenal time.

By distinguishing the two oppositions we have two dimensions of problems which arise for the phenomenological theory of perception as well as for the theory of the intentionality of consciousness in general. Lack of space forbidding, we cannot deal with the problems of both dimensions, but must confine ourselves to those which pertain to the more fundamental of the two dimensions. These are the problems related to the fact that multiple perceptions may, and do, have the same "content."

First of all, the term "content" of a perception, though only provisionally used, requires some specification. By this term we mean the *object as perceived,* that is to say the perceived object such as—but only and exactly as—it presents itself through the given perception or, what amounts to the same, the perceived object as appearing in that particular manner of one-sided adumbrational presentation in which it actually appears through the perception in question. The object as perceived or the "content" of a perception must be approached in a strictly descriptive orientation. Nothing must be attributed to or foisted into it which is not actually exhibited through the particular perception under discussion. As a consequence, the object as perceived must not be mistaken for the object *per se,* the object as it is, the real material thing. The latter can present itself in various manners of adumbrational appearance, while the term "object as perceived" refers to one particular adumbrational presentation to the exclusion of others. The real material thing possesses properties which do not fall under the present perception, though (in the case of a familiar thing) they have displayed themselves through previous perceptions, such that the present perception includes references to them. For properties of a thing to be referred to, however, is not the same as directly appearing in immediate perception. Finally, the material thing may possess unknown properties, that is to say properties which thus far have not been perceived, but under appropriate conditions are accessible to direct perceptual experience.[15] On the other hand, the object as perceived, the "content" of a perception, which in our analysis of Hume's theory proved to be different from the act of perception, must not be construed as a part, component, element, or constituent of the act. Were it a part or constituent of the act, it would obviously be involved in the same temporal change and flux as the act as a whole whose part it is.[16] That is to say, the problem of the consciousness of identity, which Hume's theory proved unable to account for, would recur unsolved. It follows that the term "content" of a perception refers to an entity *sui generis* which cannot be classified either as a psychological event nor as a real material thing.

Though the object as perceived is neither part nor constituent of the act of perception, it is most closely and intimately connected with that act. By virtue of its "content" a perception is not only a perception of a certain thing, e.g., a house rather than a tree, but also that determinate and well specified perception which it actually is, that is to say a perception through which the house presents itself under *this* aspect, from *this* side, and not in a different (though equally possible) manner of adumbrational appearance.[17] For that reason, Husserl calls the object as perceived—to be taken exactly as it appears through a given perception—the "perceptual sense" *(Wahrnehmungs-sinn)* or *perceptual noema*,[18] a term which henceforth replaces that of "content."

The notion of the noema admits of, and requires, generalization beyond the sphere of perceptual consciousness. I re-

15. Cf. Husserl, *Ideen* I §89.
16. Husserl, *Ideen* I §§41, 88, 97; *Phänomenologische Psychologie (Husserliana* vol. IX, 1962) §34.
17. Cf. Husserl, *Logische Untersuchungen* II, Halle a.d. S. M. Niemeyer, 1913–21, pp. 415 ff.; see also Marvin Farber, *The Foundation of Phenomenology,* 3rd Ed., Albany State University of New York Press, 1967, chap. XII 9.
18. Husserl, *Ideen* I pp. 182 f.

member my friend under the aspect of the opinions he
entertained in our conversation yesterday rather than under
the aspect of his professional activity or his family life. Similarly, we can think of Shakespeare as the author of *Hamlet*
or of the Sonnets or else as the director of the Globe theatre,
and the like. Quite in general, to every act of consciousness—
also denoted as *noesis*—corresponds a noema, namely an object as intended and presenting itself under a certain aspect.[19]
Again we encounter the two oppositions mentioned before: on
the one hand, the opposition between an identical noema and
multiple noeses—as when on different occasions we think of
Shakespeare as the author of *Hamlet;* on the other hand,
the opposition between Shakespeare, the real historical person
who was born in 1564 and died in 1616, and Shakespeare intended one time as the author of *Hamlet,* another time as the
author of *King Lear,* still another time as the director of the
Globe theatre, and so on.[20] Noemata, as we have seen, are
neither psychological events nor material things. Rather they
are identical and identifiable ideal entities, devoid of both
spatiality and temporality, and, of course, also of causality,
which can be shown—as we have done elsewhere [21]—to have
the same status as meanings. As usually understood, the term
"meaning" is related to verbal or, more generally, symbolic
expressions. However, the term can be so generalized as to
become synonymous with the term "sense" or noema. If it is
thus generalized, the term "meaning" denotes an object or state
of affairs of any kind, as that object or state of affairs is meant
and intended through a certain act of consciousness (perceptual or other), as the object or state of affairs presents itself to,
and stands before, the experiencing subject's mind. Meanings
in the narrower and proper sense, equivalent to signification,

19. Concerning the notions of noesis and noema in the most general sense, cf.
Husserl, *Ideen* I, Abschnitt III, chap. III.
20. Cf. Husserl, *Ideen* I, pp. 207 f.
21. A. Gurwitsch, *The Field of Consciousness* (Pittsburgh, Duquesne University
Press, 1964), Part III 5 b.

prove to form a special class of noemata or meaning in the wider sense.

The intentionality of consciousness denotes precisely the correspondence between acts as temporal psychological events and noemata as ideal atemporal entities. Hume is undoubtedly right in emphasizing the incessant temporal change and flux in which consciousness is involved. Temporality is an essential law of consciousness, but it is not its only law. The interpretation of acts of consciousness as temporal events, while correct, is incomplete insofar as these events are essentially correlated to unities of sense and meaning, in a word, noemata. We thus arrive at the *conception of consciousness as a correlation between items pertaining to two entirely different planes:* on the one hand, the plane of temporal psychological events; on the other hand, that of ideal, i.e., atemporal, meanings in the wider sense.[22] More precisely, it is a many-to-one correlation because to an indefinite multiplicity of acts or noeses there may, and does, correspond an identical noema. Differently expressed, *consciousness proves to be indissolubly—for essential reasons—connected with sense and meaning.* To every act of consciousness there corresponds, though it is not included in it as a real part or ingredient, an intentional or noematic correlate, an *intentional object* defined as *the object or state of affairs which is intended, but taken exactly and only as it is intended.* Because consciousness is a noetico-noematic correlation, the identity of the noema—as we have seen in the discussion of Hume's theory—cannot be explicitly disclosed unless the acts or noeses are at the same time rendered explicit in their temporality. Conversely—as we have shown elsewhere [23]—no account of the temporality, especially the duration, of an act of consciousness is possible except with reference to the corres-

---

22. We first presented the conception of consciousness as a noetico-noematic correlation in our article "On the intentionality of consciousness" in *Philosophical Essays in Memory of Edmund Husserl,* ed. by M. Farber (Cambridge, Harvard University Press, 1940).

23. "On the intentionality of consciousness", *loc. cit.,* pp. 80 f. and *The Field of Consciousness,* pp. 347 ff.

ponding identical atemporal noema. In the case of the duration
of an act of consciousness, the atemporality of the noema
means that the latter is not affected by the transformation
which the act undergoes when it first passes from the phase of
the "actual now" into a retentional phase ("having just been
an actual now") and then progressively recedes into a more
and more remote past, remoteness with respect to the phase
which at any given moment has the temporal character of the
"actual now".[24]

At this stage of the discussion, the advance of Husserl's
theory of intentionality over that of Brentano can be clearly
stated. According to Brentano, all psychic phenomena, and
only psychic phenomena, are characterized by the "intentional" or "mental inexistence of an object".[25] "Inexistence"
is here meant to be understood in the Latin sense of *inexis-
tentia,* existence within. Brentano also speaks, though somewhat hesitatingly, of a "relation to a content", a "direction to
an object", "an immanent object" *(immanente Gegenständlich-
keit).* Each psychic phenomenon "includes something as object
within itself, although not always in the same way. In presentation *(Vorstellung)* something is presented, in judgment something is affirmed or denied, in love [something is] loved, in
hate [something is] hated, in desire [something is] desired,
etc.". If the "intentional object" is said to be included or contained within the act or psychic phenomenon, that is to say, to
form a real part of it, or if the relation or directedness to an
object is conceived of as a phenomenal feature of the act, the

24. For the phenomenological account of duration, see Husserl, *The Phenomenology of Internal Time-Consciousness* (transl. by J. S. Churchill; Bloomington, In-
diana University Press, 1964) §§8 ff. and *Erfahrung und Urteil* §23. Both Schutz,
"William James' concept of the stream of thought, phenomenologically interpreted" *(Philosophy and Phenomenological Research* vol. I, 1941), p. 450 and
the present writer, "William James' theory of the 'transitive parts' of the stream of
consciousness" *(Philosophy and Phenomenological Research* vol. III, 1943), pp.
451 ff. have pointed out the agreement between Husserl and James concerning the
phenomenon in question.
25. F. Brentano, *Psychologie vom empirischen Standpunkt* Book II, chap. I §5;
cf. the translation by D. B. Terrel in *Realism and the Background of Phenomenology*
(ed. by R. M. Chisholm, Free Press of Glencoe, 1960), pp. 50 ff.

same problem recurs which arose in our analysis and criticism of Hume's theory. Any phenomenal feature of an act as well as any part which is contained or included in the act as one of its constituents shares the temporal fate of the act as a whole. Landgrebe [26] has pointed out that on the grounds of Brentano's theory it is hard to see how the intentional directedness of an act of consciousness can be alike or equal to that of another act, descriptively different from the first. Likeness and equality require a point of reference with respect to which they obtain. While such a point of reference is lacking in Brentano's theory, Husserl's theory provides it with the concept of the noema. Two or more descriptively different acts agree in their intentional directedness if, and only if, the same noema corresponds to all of them.

Its conception as a noetico-noematic correlation reveals the *intrinsic duality* of consciousness. This duality as intrinsic is to take the place of the *Cartesian dualism* which defines consciousness as a closed and self-contained domain, severed from whatever else there is, in the case of Descartes himself, the external world conceived as mere extendedness. Let us briefly survey a few consequences which follow from the new conception of consciousness.

First of all, the theory of Ideas must be relinquished. Considering that every act of consciousness is essentially and indissolubly connected, because correlated, with a noema, an entity of sense and meaning, it can no longer be maintained that the only direct and immediate objects of the mind are its own states, especially what has been called Ideas, understood as occurrences in the mind and psychological events. On the contrary, our direct and immediate objects are the very things, persons, states of affairs of diverse descriptions with which we are dealing, and which, through acts of consciousness, appear to us in certain manners of presentation—as they are intended

---

26. L. Landgrebe, "Husserls Phänomenologie und die Motive zu ihrer Umbildung, *Revue Internationale de Philosophie,* vol. I, 1939, p. 281.

and meant—and also in specific modes of consciousness, like the modes of perception, memory, symbolic representation, and so on. Every act of consciousness being essentially related to something other than itself which, apart from the case of acts of reflection, has a status different from that of a psychological occurrence, it follows that consciousness cannot be considered as a domain of interiority, that is to say, as self-contained and closed.

Of particular interest and importance are these consequences as they concern perceptual consciousness. As emphasized before, through an act of perception, the thing perceived appears in a certain manner of adumbrational presentation. Still, it is the thing itself which appears in bodily presence, though it presents itself one-sidedly only. A perceptual noema is not a representative of the thing perceived nor an intermediary of some sort between the perceiving subject and the thing perceived. Rather it is the very perceived thing itself as appearing under a certain aspect and from a certain side.[27] In other words, by means of perceptual experience we are in direct contact with, and have immediate access to, things and to the perceptual world at large. We are "at" the things and "at" the world. This result should be seen as deriving from Husserl's theory of intentionality rather than being ascribed to subsequent developments in existentialist philosophy. To be sure, there remain the problems concerning the transition from the particular perceptual noema to the perceived real thing which, through the given perception, appears in a certain manner of adumbrational presentation, and in thus appearing also appears as capable of presenting itself from other sides and under different aspects. However, these problems, which are of some complexity, lie outside the scope of the present discussion.

27. Husserl, *Ideen* I, §43.

Quentin Lauer, S.J.

THE PHENOMENON

OF

REASON

IN THE PEDAGOGY of the physical sciences it has become in modern times relatively easy to define, prior to scientific investigation, the particular science with which one is concerned or to which one wants to introduce students or readers. Nor does this kind of defining express merely what the individual teacher or writer *means* by a term when he uses it in a particular universe of discourse; within the scientific community there is substantial agreement as to what each science is and as to where its boundaries lie, so that the individual is not free to present it in a way which does not correspond with the common agreement. Despite certain family disputes the same is true with regard to mathematics; before beginning, one can say what one does when one does mathematics.

In regard to philosophy, however, this is not the case. Here, we might say, we cannot be told ahead of time what philosophy is, because the very doing of philosophy is a prerequisite for understanding what one is doing, and defining philosophy is itself a philosophical task, in a way in which defining science or mathematics is not a scientific or mathematical task. Nor is it self evident that the many peculiar

human activities which have at one time or another paraded
under the name of philosophy simply do not belong there,
any more than one can with certainty dispute the right of some
of our contemporaries to give philosophy a meaning of their
own and then to deny that what others call philosophizing
deserves to come under this heading.[1] But if we look at the
question historically, we can, I think, say that philosophy
began when men first sought to explain rationally what had
previously been explained by an appeal to authority, to myth,
to tradition, or simply to common opinion. By this criterion,
then, philosophy is not so much a discipline, a method, or a
body of knowledge; it is rather an attitude which human beings
bring with them in approaching the reality in the midst of
which they live. This attitude we might call a determination
to *know* reality (as opposed to opining or believing), an attitude which is philosophical, even when, as in the case of
skepticism, it results in the conviction that reality cannot be
known.[2]

Without prejudicing the issue we can, I think, say that
reality has always been looked upon as that which is present to
man when he experiences—no matter how vague and fluctuat-
ing his notion of experience may have been and no matter how
convinced many have been that reality is present as reality,
only when experience is supplemented by thought. In this con-

1. Not too many years ago a nationwide philosophical convention featured a session, entitled in the program "The Meaning of Negative Existential Statements."
In this session a group of grown men spent two hours discussing the proposition,
"There is no Santa Claus." I have serious misgivings as to whether I could engage
in such a discussion and think that I was philosophizing, but I cannot dispute the
right of others to do that sort of thing and call it philosophizing—so long as they
do not magisterially tell me that what I am doing is not philosophy.
2. There are, of course, various kinds and degrees of skepticism. Very rarely in
history has this taken the form of denying that there is knowledge, since this is
equivalent to saying, "I know that there is no knowing." Most often it takes the
form of denying that what people (or philosophers) call knowing is really knowing (in which form it constitutes a very important and necessary step, as Hegel
says, in the process of coming to know). Or it can take the Humean form of
insisting that, if one defines knowing very narrowly (on the basis of logical necessity) one will seek in vain for philosophical knowledge.

text, then, the philosophical attitude (or impulse) might tentatively be defined as the determination to understand or, better still, to grasp through reason what experience presents.[3] Such a definition, however, simply brings us face to face with another problem, which may well turn out to be the most fundamental of all philosophical problems: what is reason, or when is man being rational in his thinking? It should be fairly obvious that this question is inseparable from the question as to what is experience—neither question is answered unless both are. Neither question, however, is easily answered—it is even doubtful that they can be asked separately.

At the very beginning of his *Discourse on Method* Descartes mentions that "common sense" is the one gift of God of which no one complains that he has not been given enough.[4] This we might call the common-sense notion of common-sense (one needs a great deal of it in order to be able to admit that one does not have enough of it). By the same token there is a common-sense notion of rational thinking, and it can be somewhat crudely described as the way I think—as opposed to the way those think who disagree with me. How often in ordinary conversation do men use the expression, "It stands to reason"? The expression is admittedly not very precise, but it seems to mean at least this: "Anyone who is not prejudiced must see that my way of seeing things is correct." When we stand off from such a statement (or attitude) we can laugh at it, but behind this common-sense notion is hidden a profound truth of human experience: we do—and perhaps we must—look at our own seeing as a criterion for the way things are, or, to put it another way, *if* we really do *see* that this is the way things are, then this is the way they are, and they cannot

---

3. We can, for the moment, prescind from the question as to whether or not one can justifiably separate experience and thought. It would seem, however, that an experience which excludes thought falls short of being experience, and a thought which excludes experience is but a truncated thought.
4. *Discours de la méthode* (Adam et Tannery, Vol. VI, pp. 1–2).

correctly be seen otherwise. Human beings are often irrational, but more often than not they are so in the name of reason; they are convinced that if others would only think correctly (the way they do) they would see that this *is* the way things are—or should be (witness political thinking). Thus, professed irrationalists write books to show that the only rational thing to do is to have no confidence in reason (which nonconfidence, incidentally, is not really less rational than the confidence of the professed rationalist). The more truly rational attitude, of course, would be that which says, "My thinking is clearly not rational enough, nor will it ever become rational if it stays where it is."

Looked at historically the notion of the rational is seen in a somewhat different light. Rational thinking, we might say, begins when a distinction is made (often unconsciously) between grounds which are arbitrary and therefore unworthy of commanding human affirmation and grounds which are discernibly relevant and are therefore worthy of commanding such an affirmation. This kind of rational thinking is already present when men plow the ground and plant seed instead of simply imploring heaven for food. Such rational behavior obviously can and does exist side by side with non-rational forms of behavior—it is not even necessary that there be anything irrational about the coexistence of such forms of behavior.

Philosophy, then, begins when a conscious effort is made to explain (rather than merely to handle) reality on rational rather than on mythical, religious, or merely traditional grounds.[5] The pre-Socratics—with whom we say philosophy (Western philosophy) began—explained the world in a rational way, and this in a double sense: (1) the principles of explanation are sought in that which is to be explained (the *kosmos*); and (2) the explanation is seen as somehow im-

---

5. *What* one calls reality and *how much* of it one seeks to explain continues to be somewhat vague. Thus the first Western philosophers are called "materialists," not because this term expresses a universal theory of reality, but because the material world was all they sought to explain.

posing itself on correct thinking (however vague this latter notion may at first be). This kind of rational thinking reaches its apogee with Parmenides and Zeno, for whom the demands of thought must be affirmed, even when they apparently contradict experience or common sense.

With Socrates and Plato rational explanation is based on grounds which correct thinking cannot refuse (it is not amiss to remark that the capacity to do this kind of thinking is seen as a "divine spark" in man).[6] It is true that in the writings of Plato this kind of rationality most frequently manifests itself negatively, as again and again Socrates shows that common opinions—or opinionated opinions—have no adequate foundations. This did not mean that those opinions were not "true" (in a somewhat naive sense) but that those who held them had no adequate ground for so doing.[7] Out of this negative procedure came the conviction that the adequate ground (*aitia*) was an insight into the essence (*eidos*) of things, as distinguished from their appearances (*phainomena*). Though Plato does not develop it formally, the result of this endeavor is a "logic," i.e. a set of rules calculated to insure that thinking is adequately grounded (or to manifest that what goes under the name of thinking is not). Once again, as formal logic this sort of thing is primarily negative in its working: it does not show that thinking corresponds with reality—or that reality corresponds with thinking (Parmenides)—but it does show that a failure to think thus rigorously will make it impossible to determine whether there is such a correspondence.[8]

Logic as such appears with Aristotle (not merely in his

---

6. Cf. *Meno* 99D–100B.
7. In the naive sense an opinion is true when a proposition which is affirmed *happens* to correspond with a state of affairs. In this sense a *guess* can be true, even though the guesser has no grounds for his affirmation and doesn't really *know* whether or not it corresponds with a state of affairs. Philosophy concerns itself with such "truth" only indirectly, if at all.
8. Only late in his life (with the *Timaeus*) did Plato concern himself with the reality of the world. His primary concern throughout a long philosophical career was with the reality (or truth) of moral and political judgments. Even the universe (*kosmos*) is significant as a totality of ultimately Moral order.

Organon). It consists of a set of well-worked-out rules for determining when thinking is indeed rational. When it is, its result is *knowledge;* when it is not, its result is mere *opinion.* It might be remarked that of itself this kind of logic is quite ideal and not incompatible with the non-existence of knowledge at all—except the knowledge that the thinking itself has been correct. Even those who find fault with the Aristotelian *logic* agree with Aristotle's basic presupposition: that there are discoverable rules which are valid for *all* reasoning (at least for all that one is willing to *call* reasoning). Ideally at least (but only ideally) reason thus becomes the most universal of all universals—it can always be distinguished from what is not reason. This permitted Aristotle to hand down to posterity the most fateful of all definitions, that of man as a "rational animal." [9]

Revolutionary as he may have been in other respects—and we can scarcely call any other intervening mode of thought revolutionary in the rational sense [10]—Descartes does not change the basic Aristotelian conception of the rational. He merely changes the emphasis; with Descartes the rational becomes *more* subjective (it had always been fundamentally subjective). When the individual thinker sees things as clearly as he does in mathematical reasoning (the camel's nose) then he knows that his thinking has universal objective validity and

9. To some this definition has meant that man is a being who reasons syllogistically, à la Aristotle (though Aristotle's own conception is not nearly so narrow). To others it has meant, much more broadly, that all the activities which characterize man as man (his religion, art, science, politics, economics) must have the stamp of reason on them.
10. The advent of Christianity, it is true, produced a revolution which has influenced *all* subsequent thought (even non-Christian) in the West. Still, this was not so much a change in the manner of rational elaboration as in the manner of experiencing reality. In a very real sense Hegel was the first to realize consciously that the Christian way of experiencing changed the very concept of philosophical reasoning. Cf. *Phänomenologie des Geistes* (6th ed. Hoffmeister, Hamburg: Meiner, 1952, pp. 523–31, 544–45); *Vorlesung über die Philosophie der Religion* (ed. Glockner, II, pp. 193–94); *Vorlesungen über die Philosophie der Geschichte* (ed. Glockner, pp. 41, 378–79, 384–90, 546). Goethe chided Hegel vigorously for trying to introduce Christianity into philosophy and philosophy into Christianity (cf. Eckermann, *Gespräche mit Goethe,* Feb. 4, 1829).

that anyone who sees objectivity otherwise is not thinking rationally. The ultimate basis for Descartes' reasoning is still the going cause-effect metaphysics, and the primary opponent is authority. The ground of human assent can never be someone else's *mere* say-so; it must be the subject's own rational insight into the truth of his own assertions, secured by a tested "method" of reasoning. (To Descartes' credit, he saw that reason could not ultimately justify itself—it contains no built-in guarantee that it is not condemned to be deceived—and so he appeals to the decency of a God who would not permit man to deceive himself when acting at the summit of his potentiality.) Since it was fairly obvious, even to Descartes, that not everyone can know everything (though there was less to be known in those days), presumably there were for him ways of determining whether someone else's say-so was backed up by an adequate method of reasoning. (In contemporary thinking not every member of the scientific community personally checks whatever any other member of the community says, but there is confidence that in the long run everything will be —or has been—checked.) In any event, through the influence of Descartes the ultimate criterion of truth became the individual's own rational insight, and the model for rational investigation became the physical sciences with their mathematico-physical method—without too much concern as to whether the subject-matter under investigation lent itself to the application of such a method. The important thing was to know reality by discovering the "laws" which governed its functioning. (Only later did the assurance that one was *knowing* become more important than *what* one knew, but Descartes laid the foundations for this.)

Because Descartes emphasized both the *subjective* aspect of rational insight and the *objective* aspect of detailed experiment (as a method of arriving at rational insight), two seemingly antipodal movements arose in response to his endeavors, "rationalism" on the continent and "empiricism" across the channel. Opposed as these tendencies were, they were one in their conviction that the task of philosophy is to determine what rational thinking is and how it is to be assured, since only through rational thinking can man achieve certainty as to the truth of his affirmations.[11] Ultimately the main difference between the two camps seems to center in a somewhat pragmatic dispute over the extent to which rational certainty is achievable: the empiricists wishing to limit it to the empirically verifiable, and the rationalists wishing to set no limits at all—the apriori vs. the aposteriori approach. It was Hume who tossed a mortar shell into both camps: he narrowed the rational down to such an extent that he denied to rationalists and empiricists alike the right to think that they *know* much, if anything at all. Only if it steers clear of reality can knowledge be called "knowledge," and if it does steer clear of reality, who wants it? What is needed, then, is an effective substitute for rational knowledge, and this Hume finds in "belief." Having thoroughly undermined the old cause-effect metaphysics, which in one way or another was basic to the positions of all his predecessors, Hume left the philosophic community faced with two possibilities: either begin all over again and construct philosophy on a new base, or renounce rational certainty and be content with as high a degree of probability as unremitting and conscientious scientific effort can achieve. The first option did not wait long to materialize, and it took the form of German idealism, inaugurated by the rational critique of Immanuel Kant. The second alternative was slower in maturing, but its effects have been lasting. It produced an attitude which still dominates the scientific community and has caused a good part of the philosophical community to abridge its efforts.[12]

---

11. Cf. Franz Schnabel, *Deutsche Geschichte im 19. Jahrhundert* (Herder Taschenbuch, Freiburg, 1965, Vol. I, pp. 40–41).
12. We might add that it has resulted in a situation in which practically the whole of the scientific community and a good part of the philosophical community has lost any understanding of what the other part of the philosophical community is doing.

The reaction to Hume which we call "German Idealism" took up his challenge on two fronts: it sought to restore rational *knowledge* of reality without resorting to a cause-effect metaphysics (leaving to various forms of "materialism" the task of salvaging this sort of "realism"); and it asserted that in so doing it was achieving "scientific" knowledge. The key to these efforts can, I think, be found in the one certainty that Hume admitted (apart from rational tautologies), i.e. appearances (or phenomena), provided they were recognized as appearances, and only that.

Kant began the campaign by placing all the emphasis of his investigations on the act of knowing (he admits that his *Critique* is a preparation for philosophy, not philosophy itself).[13] If it is possible to establish the requisites for completely rational thinking, and if, when one is completely rational in one's thinking, one is knowing, then both knowing and reason have been saved. It may be, of course, that they have been saved at the cost of very severe limitations, but Kant's concern was to save knowledge, not to guarantee its relationship to reality. On one point he went along with Hume much further than his immediate successors would be willing to do; he refused to see any establishable connection between appearances and reality. In regard to "speculative" reason (which he arbitrarily identifies with theoretical reason, i.e. knowing what *is* as opposed to what *should be*) Kant feels that it can be saved, only if its content is limited to the phenomenal (appearances). In doing this, however, he is convinced that he has established the absolutely necessary laws of experience, thus enabling man to *know* how reality must *appear,* which is all that science requires, though it leaves metaphysics out in right field. The consequences have been lasting: philosophers are still trying

13. One can, of course, wonder (along with Hegel) how one guarantees the validity of philosophic reasoning without reasoning philosophically (cf. *Phänomenologie des Geistes,* Einleitung, pp. 63–64), but the problem does not seem to have bothered Kant at all.

to show how philosophy can be "scientific"—usually by jetti-
soning metaphysics. As an absolutely certain concomitant of
all experience Kant sees an awareness of the self as the central
function of experiencing (not the *ergo sum* of Descartes).
As an absolutely necessary concomitant of experiencing this
awareness of self becomes a *condition* of experiencing.[14] Logically speaking, however, a condition is a pre-condition (it is
prior to the conditioned), with the result that to speak of
knowledge is to speak of self-knowledge, the ultimate source
of all knowledge worthy of the name.

Kant's most significant followers (Fichte, Schelling, Hegel)
are united both in their negative and in their positive reaction
to Kant. Negatively they agree in refusing the radical Kantian
separation of appearance from reality (and of sense from in-
tellect), which would leave the ultimate reality of things unknown; and positively they agree that the solution to the
problem of knowing is somehow to be sought in knowledge
of the self. This solution presents itself in its most radical form
in the thought of Fichte, who seeks to derive (dialectically) all
objective knowledge of reality from knowledge of the self (he
is quite sure, incidentally, that there is extra-mental reality and
that his *Theory of Knowledge* permits him to know it). Schelling takes as his point of departure what had always been
recognized as essential, if there was to be knowledge at all, the
identity of reality as it is and reality as it is thought. Since
this kind of identity is possible, only if nature (reality) and
spirit (thought) are two sides of the same coin, Schelling
simply postulates this identity: in knowing one, one knows the
other. Knowledge of nature, however, is not *derived* from
knowledge of the self; rather the science of nature (with

---

14. This is the renowned "transcendental unity of apperception" (cf. Kant, *Kritik
der reinen Vernunft*, B132–36; Hegel, *Wissenschaft der Logik*, Hamburg: Meiner,
1963, Vol. II, p. 222), which in one way or another became the straw to which
Kant's successors clung in their efforts to reconstruct a "system" of knowledge.

which he was quite familiar) is shown to be genuinely knowledge, because it is at the same time knowledge of the self.[15]

Hegel took upon himself the enormous task of continuing, criticizing and improving upon all three of his illustrious predecessors. This he did by simultaneously affirming what they had said and negating it (thus employing the "dialectical" method of simultaneous affirmation and negation, which is at once so well known and scarcely known at all). Hegel agrees with Kant that the content of rational knowledge is provided in appearances (phenomena) which are presented in experience. He disagrees with Kant by refusing to separate these appearances from reality, knowledge from experience. He agrees with Fichte in affirming that the process of knowing (science) is dialectical in its movement and that all knowledge is ultimately self-knowledge. He disagrees with Fichte by denying that one can arrive at objective knowledge (of reality) by *beginning* with knowledge of self; one must recognize, he contends, that every step forward in the consciousness of reality is a step forward in consciousness of self—the "logical" priority of condition over the conditioned is only a red herring. Thus, though the process of knowing is indeed dialectical, the movement results in, does not start from, a knowledge of self which is identical with the knowledge of reality. Hegel agrees with Schelling in affirming the ultimate identity of reality and thought reality (nature and spirit). He disagrees with Schelling by insisting that this identity cannot be a point of departure—which would be empty of content and out of which no amount of effort could carve a content. Rather, this identity is only gradually revealed in a painstaking passage from the first awareness of objectivity in sense perception to the ultimate knowledge of all this initial step implies (phenomenology),

---

15. Hegel (*Phänomenologie*, pp. 17–18; cf. 180–81) calls this a subterfuge: simply taking what is already considered to be known and throwing over it the cloak of "scientific system," without ever showing that the system is genuinely scientific.

which knowledge can then be filled out by working in the opposite direction, i.e. from general to particularized knowledge (logic). We shall grasp Hegel's gigantic effort to solve the dilemma of thought vs. reality, only if we see how he grasped the Humean (and Kantian) bull squarely by the horns. He will begin where Hume says one must begin, with the certainty of appearances (phenomena), but he will go where Hume said one cannot go, to a knowledge of reality, because he refuses to separate appearances from reality. Sense perception is not distinct from knowledge; it is the beginning of a process, the whole of which ultimately reveals itself to be knowledge. The cause-effect metaphysics, which, along with Hume and Kant, he rejects, had seen appearances as produced by and revelatory of reality—and as produced by, therefore separate from, the reality which they reveal. Rather than try to put this Humpty-Dumpty together again, Hegel will see the appearing of reality as integral to the being of reality, and the process of working this out he will call "phenomenology" —not in the sense that phenomena provide all the evidence that is needed for grasping the "essence" of reality, but in the sense that the total process of experience is identical with the total process of knowledge.

In recent years the term "phenomenology" has become familiar to even those who merely dabble in philosophy. What the term really signifies, however, is familiar to relatively few, whether it is used in the contemporary Husserlian or in the earlier Hegelian sense. Although it would not be without value to compare the two uses of the term (and the disciplines which they designate)—seeing how they differ and how, in some ways, they supplement each other—we shall have to content ourselves here with a description of the Hegelian phenomenology, hoping that its efforts to solve the riddle of the relationship between experience and reason may contribute to an understanding of phenomenology in its other manifestations.

Although it is true that the name "philosophy" has been

reserved for that which is preeminently a rational discipline, and though history has accorded the title "philosopher" only to those who have contributed to the rational elaboration of human experience, it is equally true that the greatness of the *great* Philosophers does not rest on the inner consistency or on the convincing power of such rational elaborations. Rather, their greatness consists (as does that of the great poet or great artist) in the quality of their experience, its capacity to reveal in a new way the possibilities of human experience. The analyses and explanations which the philosopher provides are precisely the provisional in his contribution, but they do serve to point up the significance of the experience to which he is a witness and whereby he leaves his mark on the experiences of those who come after him. Although we continue to marvel at the monumental rational structures they have bequeathed to us, the influence of a Plato or an Aristotle, a Kant or a Hegel, even of a Husserl or a Wittgenstein, is not to be discovered in these structures but in the profundity of an experience, which the penetration of their philosophical genius has made possible and which the lucidity of their elaboration has enabled them to communicate. Their experience, in its turn, is not significant because it is experience—as though this were some sort of universal for which a unified "logic" could be prescribed— but because it is the experience of a genius, whose capacity for experience is in a very special way his own. We can say, I think, that each great philosopher has had a very special way of experiencing experience through which he has enriched the sum-total of human experience.

Applying this to the Hegelian manner of experiencing, we can, I think, say that it is characterized by an extraordinary confidence in reason. This is obviously opposed to the "romantic" glorification of emotion and intuition, which Hegel constantly characterized as an unwarranted short-cut to knowledge. Not so obviously but equally vigorously it is opposed to the sentimental rationalism of the "Enlightenment," which first deified human reason and then knelt down in adoration before it.[16] Nor, finally, was it the confidence of a Kant or a Fichte, who purchased their confidence by handing over to faith the ultimate concerns of human living and limited reason to mundane considerations.[17] Hegel's was rather the confidence of a Plato or an Aristotle, who saw reason as that which in the highest degree distinguishes man as man and which should, therefore, characterize man when he is engaged with that which is of the highest interest to him. Like those who went before him Hegel saw reason as infallible in the sense that what reason saw to be true simply had to be true; and, like those who went before him, he saw reason as absolutely one, in the sense that what any human reason saw to be necessarily true had to be true for any other reason which was truly reason. This conviction, of course, was properly speaking a pre-philosophical conviction—neither strictly speaking self evident nor philosophically verifiable. It was not, then, the starting point of Hegel's philosophizing, but it did influence his whole manner of thought, never letting him rest, until his painstaking pursuit of experience should lead him to a reason which, he felt, had shown itself to be one and infallible in the very process that experience goes through in becoming reason. Whether or not we think that this pursuit has been successful depends on the judgment we make after we have followed Hegel through the tortuous intricacies of his *Phenomenology of Spirit*.

As we said before, characteristic of any phenomenology (except the negative sort which preceded Hegel's, remnants of which are still detectable in Kant's thought) [18] is the conviction that philosophy must not only begin in experience but

16. Cf. *Phänomenologie*, p. 388.
17. Cf. "Glauben und Wissen" (unveränderter Abdruck aus: *G. Wilh. Fr. Hegel, Erste Druckschriften*, Leipzig: Meiner, 1928), Hamburg: Himmelheber, 1962, pp. 2, 6, 14.
18. Cf. *Phänomenologie* (Einleitung des Herausgebers), pp. VII–XVII; Kant, *Kritik der reinen Vernunft* (B86) calls ancient dialectic a "logik des Scheins," and (B87) transcendental dialectic a "Kritik des dialektischen Scheins"; cf. B349–50.

must never become detached from experience, if it is not to
lose itself in unwarranted "rational" vagaries.[19] There are,
however, two characteristics which mark the Hegelian concept
of experience and which distinguish it from those conceptions
of experience which are current in most of the "phenomenolo-
gies" inspired by Husserl. For Hegel whatever is inevitably
implied in any experience (it never stands still) is integral to
that experience in its totality, no matter how far it may advance
beyond the merely empirical. In accord with this, reason is not
distinct from experience; it is not even the result of experience;
reasoning is simply the highest form of experiencing. Secondly,
experience is historical, not merely in the sense that it develops
(each experience conditioning each subsequent experience),
but also in the more profound sense that human history is
integral to human experience and that the great events of human history are landmarks in the progress of human experience, as the spirit advances toward full consciousness of what
it is to be spirit. We can illustrate the difference at this point
with but one telling example. Not only was Hegel as a 19th-
century man impressed by the enormous historical significance
of the French Revolution (as were all his thinking contemporaries), but as a philosopher he saw in it the most significant
contemporary phenomenon in the steady march of the human
spirit throught history (the first practical attempt in history to
build a political community founded on a rationally conceived
idea of man as such and of his essential freedom). For Hegel
any attempt to philosophize in abstraction from the French
Revolution was a refusal to be "timely" in one's thinking and,
therefore, a refusal really to philosophize.[20] On the other hand,
Husserl experienced World War I more immediately than did

---

19. Hegel was unalterably opposed to what he called "rationalism": "In regard to
both content and form rationalism is contrary to philosophy," *Vorlesungen über
die Geschichte der Philosophie* (ed. Glockner), I, p. 112.
20. Cf. Joachim Ritter, *Hegel und die französische Revolution* (Frankfurt/M:
Suhrkamp, 1965).

Hegel the French Revolution. We may assume that, as a man, Husserl saw in it the end of an era in human thinking and human living. So far as I have been able to determine, however, there is no evidence that, as a philosopher, he ever thought of it at all; in his sense of the term it had simply no significance for "phenomenology." It may have been integral to human experience (though one doubts that he saw this); it had nothing to do with philosophical experience.[21]

All this is said, not by way of criticizing Husserl who had his own reasons for not according the "contingent" any philosophical significance, but in order that we may better understand the phenomenology of Hegel, rooted as it is in the whole of human experience, not merely in his own or that of his associates or, for that matter, in that of philosophers as a whole. Nor is it concerned with some sort of abstraction, simply labeled "experience." The *Phenomenology of Spirit* is historical, not in the ordinary sense of presenting a chronological record of a series of events (it is not chronological at all), but in the sense that it sees the whole of human history as important for the development of human consciousness, and in the sense that we shall not understand man until we have examined the various forms which this developing consciousness has taken in the course of history—even though Hegel does not examine them in the order in which they occurred (they keep recurring). Nor is the *Phenomenology* a history of philosophy. It seeks to take into account all the forms of human consciousness which have been manifested in the course of history, through which and in which spirit gradually comes

---

21. It would not have been impossible for Husserl to have initiated a "phenomenology of love" or a "phenomenology of religion," in so far as these are phenomena which can be analysed, investigated, explained, and whose "essence" can be discovered. It would, however, have been quite impossible for Husserl to look upon love or religion as experiences of the human spirit and, as such, integral to the very process of philosophizing. Among "Husserlian phenomenologists" the nearest approach to this sort of thing is to be found in the works of Max Scheler, e.g. *On the Eternal in Man.*

to a realization that all history is its history. Though it is difficult to follow him in this, it is Hegel's contention that, if we begin with the simplest of all experiences, that of a single individual faced with an unrelated object of sense consciousness, we shall find that this simple act of consciousness demands for its elucidation—or self-elucidation—the whole process of human consciousness, not only on the individual but also on the social and historical levels.

It is generally admitted that Hegel's *Phenomenology of Spirit* is one of the great masterpieces of philosophical literature (although not too many can say why). It is also admitted, even by those who know it best, that it is one of the most difficult of all the works in this literature. For many, of course, the main difficulty is to be found in the language which Hegel employs, and since they rarely get beyond this they excuse themselves from the kind of effort which would bring them face to face with the true difficulty of following it through. It is difficult because of the enormous philosophical, literary, cultural, and historical erudition needed in order merely to enter into its universe of discourse. It is difficult to habituate oneself to the involuted style of writing and to the peculiar use of concepts which one may have thought familiar. It is difficult because its contents reflect Hegel's own vast erudition, which he somehow sought to squeeze between the covers of one book. But the chief difficulty of all is that of staying with the method from beginning to end and trying to understand why the author thinks that every step necessarily implies every other.[22] If we do make the effort, however, though we may not at the end be convinced that Hegel has fully proved his point, we shall not be likely to think that the torture was in vain.

From Descartes to Fichte those who sought to guarantee the validity of human reasoning were in search of some indubitable truth or principle from which the movement of

---

22. Cf. *Phänomenologie*, Einleitung des Herausgebers, p. VI.

knowing could begin and which would be the constant support of all knowledge derived from it. For Hegel, on the contrary, it is a matter of indifference whether we begin with truth or error, since a beginning (precisely because it is a beginning) is never either 100 per cent true or 100 per cent false. The important thing is that we begin and that we then follow with the utmost fidelity the movement of successive implication which this initial act of consciousness involves. Even error will imply its own truth, because as an act of consciousness it carries within itself, so to speak, its own built-in corrective (one is reminded of the rational optimism of Peirce, James, Dewey). It is precisely this inner principle of truth in all consciousness, however, thoroughly distinct as it is from the subjective certainty one has regarding the object of consciousness, which makes the movement of the *Phenomenology* so difficult to follow. It is, on the other hand, this conviction of the truth in all consciousness which permits Hegel to take the somewhat discredited title of "phenomenology" and apply it to his own approach to philosophical knowing. In the German tradition which preceded Hegel, *appearances* had always been suspect because of their capacity to deceive, and phenomenology had been a method of detecting the fallacy of appearances and thus avoiding deception. Hegel, however, looks upon appearances as the bearers of truth, so long as the unremitting effort of thinking permits them to purify themselves of the element of error which is inseparable from partial truth.

If, then, science is the methodical procedure through which human thinking moves in arriving at a grasp of truth, we can understand why Hegel calls science the movement we have so summarily described. Its goal is knowing—Hegel calls it "absolute knowing"—but science is not merely the knowing; it is the whole process of coming to know. Short of the *whole* process there is no science. It is for this reason that Hegel calls his *Phenomenology* a "science"—the original title had been *Wissenschaft der Erfahrung des Bewusstseins* ("science of the experience of consciousness"). It should be remarked, incidentally, that he does not intend it as a science whose object is consciousness (a sort of psychology), but rather as a science which consists in consciousness going through the process of its experiencing. It is a science, precisely because the movement of experience is itself scientific (only when, of course, arbitrary subjective associations have been eliminated and none but the inevitable implications of consciousness are allowed to assert themselves). Reality *appears* in consciousness, and the series of these appearings is *experience*. This does not mean that what appears is some sort of reality behind the appearing (as it is for Kant), but rather that appearing is what reality does when it truly is. Thus, just as the shining of light is not something other than light, the appearing of reality is not something other than reality. If the appearing is cut short at any stage in the process it is not the true being of reality. This last is what most clearly distinguishes the Hegelian from the Husserlian phenomenology; only in the total process of appearing is reality discoverable as what it is, and what it is is not some "essence" contained *in* the appearing; it is the sum-total of appearing as process.[23]

We have now reached the point, I think, where we can see all this illustrated in the text of Hegel's *Phenomenology of Spirit*. It is the record of the experience of consciousness, and as such it is historical in character—although, as we said, it does not present a historical account in the sense in which we have come to understand that term. It is also "systematic," in the sense that it is a gigantic effort to put order into the totality

---

23. Obviously this should not be taken to mean that the "essence" is *not* grasped in the process. In so far as the essence is present to consciousness, it too is *experienced*. It is significant, however, that for Hegel knowledge of essence is only a stage along the way toward the fullness of knowledge (cf. *Wissenschaft der Logik*, II, pp. 213–14).

182 QUENTIN LAUER, S.J.

of forms in which human experiencing has manifested itself.[24] But the "system" is not a preestablished framework into which the sum of experiences is made to fit; [25] rather it is an order, which we may frequently have difficulty in recognizing as order, of the forms which the human spirit takes in passing from minimal consciousness to the fullness of knowledge. This is not, be it remarked again, a passage from experience to knowledge; the whole movement is experience—even to know is to experience knowing (just as to love is to experience loving). If we are to know science, then, science must appear (in Hegel's terms it must be an *Erscheinung*), but the appearing of science is not other than the being of science, any more than the appearing of pain (its being experienced) is other than pain.[26]

The process begins with simple, naive, immediate consciousness of a sensible object (the Humean paradigm of all consciousness), which is no sooner present than it reveals to itself that it is not the knowledge it thought it was.[27] In order to pass beyond this eminently unsatisfactory stage consciousness must negate its own inadequacy, which is but another way of saying that it must negate the immediacy (and "cer-

24. Cf. Walter Kaufmann, *Hegel* (New York: Doubleday, 1965), pp. 146–49. One gets the impression in reading the *Phenomenology* that Hegel's head was just bursting with the erudition he had gathered over the years and whose significance he had meditated profoundly.
25. Just the reverse would seem to be the case. Hegel was convinced that all the forms of experience he had collected were significant; the task was to put them into some sort of order which would bring out this significance.
26. The example is taken from Locke, who seems to have been on the brink of a discovery similar to Hegel's. Unfortunately, however, he did not carry this insight beyond its application to the perception of sensible qualities.
27. In what follows we shall attempt to present the thought movement of Hegel in a language which will (hopefully) make up in familiarity for what it loses in technical accuracy. Those who are familiar with Hegel's text should have no difficulty recognizing the details in the broad outlines of this summary. One must, of course, bear in mind that an interpreter can scarcely avoid reducing Hegel's thought to the limits of his own understanding. The fact that an interpreter's principles do not permit him to understand Hegel's principles does not necessarily speak against Hegel. Any fool can to his own satisfaction make a fool out of Hegel.

tainty") which makes it satisfied to stand still where it is.[28]
Thus, at the very beginning, the mainspring of the process is
introduced as negation, negating that immediacy which we
might call experience's dead-end street, and which Hegel qualifies as "abstract." In this sense the process will be throughout
a negative one; it will be process at all only to the extent that
consciousness repeatedly denies itself the illusory satisfaction
of clinging to the certainty which immediacy promises but
never gives. Hegel is convinced that, if we follow this negative
process conscientiously, it will repeatedly reveal its further
positive content and will not let us stop until it has become
knowledge in the truest and fullest sense of the term (one
suspects, of course, that he was convinced of this *before* he
went through the process, but he is content nevertheless to let
the process speak for itself). The point is that the degree of
certainty in consciousness is in inverse proportion to its content, and that the significance of knowledge is in direct proportion to its content, not to the certainty we have regarding
it.[29] Of course, if *all* this meant only a progressive loss of certainty, the knowledge at which Hegel aims would turn out to
be empty. Rather it means a progressive regaining of certainty
in the realization that the immediate certainty of sense consciousness is sterile without the mediation of thought. The
fatal mistake, Hegel feels, is the opinion that to *think* what

---

28. Hume had recognized the negative character of the process whereby consciousness goes from the immediacy of sense impressions to the mediacy of thought.
Since for him, however, sense impression was the paradigm of consciousness, the
movement in question was purely negative, betokening a *loss* in concreteness and,
therefore, in validity. Hegel, as we shall see, moves in exactly the opposite direction: the more immediate, the more abstract; the process of mediation (negation
of immediacy) is a process of concretization.
29. Hegel is not opposed to abstraction; he recognizes it as a necessary step in
human thinking (cf. *Phänomenologie*, p. 29). Abstraction makes the real unreal
(mental), but it does so in order to reinstate reality at a higher level. It is characteristic of his thought (even in the *Logik*) that he sees reason as primarily concerned with concrete reality, not with necessary (abstract) judgments. The bond
between abstractness (usually triviality) and certainty has not ceased, even in our
day, to be a close one.

was at first only sensibly perceived is to introduce an element foreign to the reality which is perceived.[30] Thinking is foreign neither to sensation nor to reality; it is integral to the process in which alone both are what they *really* are. Hegel is further convinced that in conscientiously observing this process of experiencing we will see that thought is integral to it, i.e. that thought reality is more real than reality which is not thought.[31]

Hegel is as aware as is anyone else that thinking is an operation of the subject who thinks. Where he differs from others is in insisting that it is at the same time an activity of the object which is thought,[32] if it is truly thought and not merely imagined or represented. This can be illustrated by a simple example which Hegel himself gives. When we say that one thing is distinguished from another, we are saying that the one distinguishes itself from the other, in the sense that the one really has a character or determination which is different from what the other has and which makes the one really different from the other. Determination, however, is that whereby things are manifest to consciousness as this or that. Thus, the determinations of things are at one and the same time in things and in the consciousness one has of things (in this case in *thought*). At the same time difference *from* another is relation *to* another, and relation is inseparable from thought. When the thought which relates one thing to another as different is true thought, then, the two things are really different from each other.

Thought, then, means initially the effort to "understand" what is thought, and Hegel sees the effort to understand as an effort to explain why things are experienced the way they are

---

30. Cf. *Phänomenologie*, pp. 63–64.
31. This, in somewhat more modern dress, reiterates the insight of Plato who saw more genuine reality in "ideas" than he did in sense impressions.
32. Heidegger, with his flare for manipulating language, has partially recaptured this in speaking of "the thinking of Being" (*das Denken des Seins*), where the "of" governs "Being" as both an objective *and* a subjective genitive—when man thinks Being, it is Being which thinks.

(he feels that this is as far as Kant went). This effort manifests itself in the positing of some hidden "essence" or "force" within things, which explains their being outwardly the way they appear (the example is taken from Newtonian physics). If, however, this "essence" or "force" is outside consciousness it will be thoroughly sterile, since it cannot explain what is *in* consciousness (short of an indemonstrable cause-effect relationship). Once more, then, consciousness makes the effort to overcome sterility, and this carries it beyond understanding, at the same time revealing the inadequacy of considering only the object of consciousness; consciousness must turn to an examination of itself, and this is self-consciousness.[33]

At this point the *Phenomenology of Spirit* becomes really difficult, and the difficulty increases as we continue in our efforts to follow the movement of self-experiencing consciousness which it describes. Just as on the level of mere objective consciousness there was a first immediate stage which revealed itself as inadequate to its own object, so here on the level of self-consciousness there is a first immediate stage, which we can call the stage of individual self-consciousness, which in turn reveals itself as inadequate and relatively sterile.[34] That the individual be genuinely conscious of himself he must be conscious of being recognized as a self, which recognition he can find only in other selves, whom he in turn recognizes as selves.[35] Not only is coming to consciousness of self a process,

---

33. The danger of superficiality in making this jump so rapidly is obvious. We should not forget that this whole negative process is a "struggle," a "torture." Cf. *Phänomenologie*, pp. 12–13.
34. Obviously any but the very first step in the process is not fully immediate, only relatively so, i.e. relatively to the fullness of the consciousness achieved on any level and to the (absolute) fullness of consciousness which is revealed only at the end. Self-consciousness, however, can be considered immediate in that very first relation to its object whereby it turns away from the object to itself. This first step, Hegel tells us, is mediated through "desire," since in this relation to its object the subject is revealed to itself.
35. The whole section of the *Phenomenology* entitled "Self-Consciousness" has something of the character of a digression—but a necessary digression. Objective consciousness is revealed as truly objective only when it is also consciousness of self (cf. "transcendental unity of apperception"), but this requires that self-con-

it is a long process and, like the process we have already seen, it is a process of mediation (negation). Experience has already found that consciousness of objects is empty without the mediation of thought originating in the subject; now it will find that consciousness of self is little more than the grasp of another kind of object, when it is not supplemented by the mediation involved in the mutual recognition accorded in a community of selves.[36]

From here on, then, the individual, even as an individual, cannot progress by merely experiencing its own experience; it must take in the experience of others and not stop until its own experience blends with the collective experience of humanity (in its history). Thus it is that the Hegelian phenomenology becomes historical in a way that no contemporary phenomenology is (including that of Heidegger, Sartre, Merleau-Ponty, or even Scheler). Man begins to recognize himself progressively for what he really is, a rational being whose grasp of reality is identified with the autonomy of his own conceptual life. Consciousness of rationality, then, goes hand in hand with consciousness of freedom, neither of which is present on the level of merely "natural" (naive) consciousness, but is acquired in the process of becoming a "human" consciousness, or in the process of developing into spirit, as opposed to mere nature. Later, when he looks back from a different vantage point, Hegel will be able to entitle his work a *Phenomenology of Spirit;* up to the present point he can know only that it is still a "Science of the Experience of Consciousness."

sciousness be given its full significance, which means far more than that the individual have himself as the object of his consciousness. It is far from easy to grasp that a self (essentially *subject*) should be the *object* of consciousness; it is impossible, if the only self there is to grasp is one's own. This sort of self-consciousness requires a complex movement of mutual recognition, in which subjects are to each other both objects and subjects.

36. Negation, for Hegel, is never merely mutual opposition. To say that the subject as *other* than the object is the negative of the object is not to say that the negative of the subject is merely the object as other; there would be no *movement* in this. Rather the significant negative of the subject must be another other, i.e. another subject.

Consciousness has now begun to experience itself as free (autonomous, self-determined). But as an immediate experience of freedom (or an experience of immediate freedom) consciousness experiences not true freedom but only independence, which immediately reveals itself as independence *of* others, and this on careful examination turns out to be dependence *on* others—the "of" means a necessary relation *to* others and manifests the meaninglessness of freedom in isolation *from* others. Man is free only in community *with* other men, which by implication means that man is rational only in common with other men, not as isolated (even in thought) from them.[37] Hegel was never willing to see genuine freedom in mere freedom of thought (whether in the form of stoicism, skepticism, the Enlightenment, or Romanticism—"stone walls do not a prison make"). More often than not (as Marx saw so well) freedom of thought is a poor substitute for the effort to *realize* freedom in action (its result in our own day is that the best heads are not doing the most important thinking— they are producing the instruments which can destroy the world).[38]

Historically speaking the search for an adequate guarantee of individual reason (from Descartes to Fichte) has been unable to survive the rejection of the cause-effect metaphysics. If the activity of a cause cannot guarantee the universal validity of reason's conclusions, then the guarantee (if such there be) must come from elsewhere, and the only answer to this seems to be some sort of idealism, where thinking finds within itself

37. Franz Schnabel has pointed out how German scholars in the 19th century were encouraged to great freedom of thought (in science) to keep them from realizing their lack of political freedom. Cf. *Deutsche Geschichte im 19. Jahrhundert,* V, p. 160.
38. It is conceivable that an abstract consideration of man might reveal that all men are essentially free. It is doubtful, however, that such a consideration could reveal that those who are *de facto* not free (e.g. the so-called "primitive" peoples) are men in the full sense. It is not by "thinking about" them but by being "related to" them that we discover concrete men—though even the inadequacies of abstract thinking can prompt us to seek such relatedness.

the guarantee of its own validity. Hegel's point is that reason
will never acquire this guarantee of universal validity, if all it
is is individual reason (an abstract universalization of which,
à la Kant or Fichte, is no more than an assertion of universality, not a guarantee). It is all very well to say that what I
rationally know to be true is necessarily true for everyone who
reasons correctly, but Hegel will see things in the reverse
order: if common reason (the reason of man as such) prescribes that things be seen in a certain way, then it prescribes
that my individual reason see things the same way. The problem, however, is not to see that this is the case; it is rather to
know when it is common reason which speaks (just as Rousseau's problem, which he never solved, was to know when the
"general will" speaks). Hegel's search, then, is for something
(by way of example) whose validity is the product of the community and not of any individual member of the community.[39]
Once more he borrows a page from Rousseau and finds this
common product in *law* (involving, of course, a somewhat
idealized picture of democracy according to which its laws, if
genuinely laws, are in truth legislated by the whole of the people). Actually Hegel realizes that, if this is seen merely on the
level of positive law, the picture is far too ideal ever to be true.
When he contemplates the moral law, however, he finds an
initial realization of that which is a product of reason and still
not a product of the individual, except to the extent that the
individual really sees that in so thinking both he and others are
thinking the same.

But even this realization, which in principle is justified,
has its concrete vicissitudes. What one would merely like to
be true can present itself as having the kind of universality

---

39. It would require another lecture to show that reasoning in the sense in which
it here begins to be understood cannot be separated from effective action (eco-
nomic, social, political). Cf. Herbert Marcuse, *Reason and Revolution,* (New
York: Oxford University Press, 1941). Suffice it to remark here that the concept
of active reason is not a Marxist monopoly.

desired. Sentiment, too, can readily parade in the garb of reason. In short, there can be any number of attempts to universalize private opinion—and each attempt must manifest its inadequacy (the negative process), if there is to be progress toward true universality. The solution is not to be found in the abstract community of human nature (practical experience discredits this); [40] nor is it to be found in a merely empirical observation of what men *de facto* think and do. It comes rather in the recognition that the rational is purposeful activity and that purpose is meaningful only if it is concretely the purpose for which all exist. In the order of mere vital nature, where activity is unconsciously and thoroughly determined, this is not too difficult to see; the purpose of the things of nature is what in fact through their activity they do become. On the level of spiritual activity, however, the difficulty is almost insurmountable, because it involves steering a middle course between what actually *is* done (pure empiricism) and what simply *should be* done (pure idealism), a course which can be successfully steered only if both are reconciled in a purpose prescribed by a reason which is at once superior to any individual reason and yet not separable from individual reason, when it truly functions as reason. [41]

The answer to this dilemma Hegel finds in his concept of spirit, and it is precisely here that it is most difficult to follow him, not in the sense of understanding what he says (though that is difficult enough), but in the sense of going along with him. He has seen that all efforts to make individual thinking a

---

40. Man, according to Hegel, is not by nature good (no more than he is by nature free)—though he might conceivably be by nature "innocent." Man must *become* good, and this involves a negation of mere nature, just as does becoming *rational*.
41. Here those who would make of Hegel an atheist run up against a hurdle which they much too facilely overleap. One can, of course, say that, for Hegel, the supreme principle is *Geist,* and that *Geist* is not God. Since, however, *Geist* is clearly not reducible to *mind* or to any function or sum-total of functions of the individual, and since it can be treated as an abstraction only if one does violence to the texts, it seems clear enough that, negatively at least, his conception of *Geist* would be equally unacceptable to an atheist as would be God. Feuerbach, Marx, and Engels, at least, had the good sense to see this.

valid paradigm for all thinking have failed. What is left, then, is that the thinking of all should be the paradigm for individual thinking, which it can be, if the thinking of the individual can be concretely identified with the thinking of all. What thinks in this way, Hegel tells us, is spirit, and consciousness is raised to this level of thinking by going through all the stages we have observed—and then some.[42] As an illustration of spirit he takes what is frequently (more frequently in his day) called the spirit of a people, a way of thinking which belongs to each because first of all it belongs to all. On this level, however, there is an element of unconsciousness in the unity of thinking which has been achieved.[43] But if the same degree of unity which is observed on this level can be consciously achieved on another level, then we are a lot closer to what we are seeking. Hegel feels that this kind of unity can be achieved, not in a people, but in a state which is truly a state (the qualification, of course, makes it somewhat abstractly ideal). The point is, however, that Hegel is seeking a situation where community of thought is the guarantee of its validity rather than one in which the validity of thought is the guarantee of its community, a conception of democracy which escaped even Rousseau— and certainly Marx—requiring as it does a confidence in the people which few share.[44] The situation may be unjustifiably

---

42. The whole discussion of religion, which in fact repeats the overall progress of spirit through history, is integral to this "science of experience."

43. Much of Hegel's "unhistorical" swinging backwards and forwards can be explained by his search for illustrations of steps in the process. Here he goes back to the Greeks, though chronologically he had already passed far beyond them.

44. It is the rare philosopher indeed who says, as Hegel does, that the people as a whole cannot be fooled: "When the general question is asked, *whether it is permissible to deceive a people* (Frederick the Great), the answer must in fact be that the question is pointless, while in this it is impossible to deceive a people" (*Phänomenologie,* p. 392).

This, of course, applies specifically to faith, but in another place Hegel accords even a certain speculative infallibility to an *organized* common thinking: "To Jacobi's remark that the systems are an organized non-knowing we need only add that non-knowing—the cognition of individuals—becomes knowing by the very fact that it is organized" ("Differenz der Fichteschen und Schellingschen Systems der Philosophie," *Erste Druckschriften,* ed. G. Lasson, Leipzig: Meiner, 1928, p. 86).

utopian in its conception, but there is no question that, *if* achieved, it would be far more concrete than its opposite. To a great extent we do, in fact, attribute a greater validity to a community of experience than we do to isolated experience. If there are ways in which the experiences of each can be consciously related to the experiences of each other and of all, there is hope that the interrelatedness of all experience (rooted in the genuineness of total human interrelatedness) will have a validity which merely individual experience can never have.[45]

Universal experience, of course, will be just as meaningless as individual experience, if it does not have a content. Hegel's claim, however, is that it does have a content, a content which we shall grasp if we follow him conscientiously through the successive stages he has described for us, a description, we might say, which constitutes a run-down of all the forms which experience (and thinking) has taken in the course of its long history. Not only is it difficult to conceive of a basic human attitude which is not presented here (however metaphorically), but no one of them is held up merely as a curiosity; each is seen as a contribution to the onward march.[46] As Hegel presents these forms, they seem to tumble over each other in rich confusion (scarcely systematically) and leave us with one big headache. If we really read the *Phenomenology,* however, we can say that we have seen everything; it will be up to us to make something of what we have seen. It may be that we shall not make of it what Hegel did—the triumphant march toward rationality and self-determination—but, one way or another,

45. Thus, the whole question of "intersubjectivity" is not for Hegel an afterthought (as it seems to be for Husserl, who feels the need of concretizing a universal subjectivity which is clearly abstract). Intersubjective relatedness is integral to the process of human experience becoming reason.
46. Most of the forms of spirit which Hegel describes have names which have been taken from historical movements, e.g. stoicism, skepticism, enlightenment. They are not, however, to be confined to these time-conditioned phenomena; each is a form which appears again and again.

the whole will do something to our way of philosophizing; one is never the same after a careful reading of Hegel. But, one should not read him at all, if one is unwilling that philosophy be a risk. Philosophy as Hegel conceives it is hard work—if one insists on always being in charge, it is impossible work.[47]

---

47. Cf. *Phänomenologie,* p. 57.

Walter Kaufmann

THE RIDDLE OF

OEDIPUS:

TRAGEDY AND PHILOSOPHY

THE IDEA OF THE Arnold Isenberg Memorial Lectures is beautiful. As soon as I was invited to participate in the first year's series, I thought of "Tragedy and Philosophy" as a singularly appropriate title for my contribution.[1] Since then, Prentice-Hall has published *Aesthetic Theories,* edited by Karl Aschenbrenner and Arnold Isenberg; and this volume includes selections from both Aristotle's *Poetics* and Nietzsche's *Birth of Tragedy.* Tragedy is the art on which great philosophers have written most: besides Aristotle and Nietzsche, also Plato, Hume, and Schopenhauer—and more recently, Max Scheler, Karl Jaspers, and Martin Heidegger. I shall not go out of my way to link my ideas to those of the last three men, or even to Nietzsche's, although this lecture has been lumped with some

---

1. In 1962/63 I was asked to lecture on "Literature and Philosophy" at The He-brew University in Jerusalem, devoted most of my course to Greek tragedy, and decided to work up my ideas into a book. Invited to give an Isenberg Memorial Lecture, I decided to make use of some of this material. My ideas are developed much more fully in my *Tragedy,* published by Doubleday and Company, Copyright © 1968 by Walter Kaufmann.

As far as it is convenient, references are given in the text, to hold down the number of the footnotes. In the case of modern books, Arabic figures refer to pages; in the case of ancient poetry, to lines.

others under the general heading of "Phenomenology and Existentialism." Let it suffice that I share common concerns with some phenomenologists and existentialists—and with Arnold Isenberg.

My title, "The Riddle of *Oedipus*," is ambiguous. Although I shall venture a suggestion about the riddle of the Sphinx, I shall concentrate on the riddle posed by Sophocles' *Oedipus Tyrannus:* I shall try to make a contribution to the interpretation of this tragedy—and not only of *this* tragedy. It is a commoplace—and what is more, it is also true—that Aristotle's uniquely influential theory of tragedy is based preeminently on his reading of Sophocles' *Oedipus Tyrannus;* and I shall contest this reading and propose a different reading of the play and a more philosophical approach to literature, using *Oedipus Tyrannus* as a paradigm case.

1.

Aristotle's classical interpretation of the play is immensely suggestive. Let us first consider a few passages in his *Poetics* in which *Oedipus* is not mentioned explicitly—passages in which we nevertheless encounter generalizations about tragedy that appear to be based on this play.

Aristotle distinguishes six formative elements of tragedy—plot, character, thought, diction, melody, and spectacle—and goes on to say, in Chapter 6, that the plot is in a sense more important than the characters, because the characters are required by the action, not vice versa. So far, his observation seems true of the extant tragedies of both Aeschylus and Sophocles, not merely of *Oedipus Tyrannus,* though it seems notably inapplicable to, say, Shakespeare's *Hamlet.* The perennial fascination of *Prometheus* and the *Oresteia, Antigone* and *Oedipus Tyrannus, Philoctetes* and *Electra* is due to what Aristotle calls their plots. (The Greek word he uses is *mythos,* and it may be tempting to insist on the truth of his statement, even if it is taken to refer to the myths rather than the plots. But I shall try to show later on that this is a common error of considerable significance.) The unique fascination of *Hamlet,* on the other hand, is due largely to the character of the hero, much less to Shakespeare's plot. Shakespeare's characters, like Dostoevsky's, have an inveterate tendency to reach out far beyond the plot and its immediate requirements: they become interesting as individuals. They say things not required by the story line, and our attitudes toward them are shaped much more by speeches of that sort than by the central action—especially in *Hamlet,* but also in *Macbeth.* This is one of the most striking differences between Shakespeare on the one hand and Aeschylus and Sophocles on the other.

When Aristotle goes on, however, still in Chapter 6, to say that the plot works through reversals and recognitions, this is no longer a sound generalization about Aeschylus and Sophocles but probably suggested mainly by his admiration for *Oedipus Tyrannus.* To mention only two of the very greatest of Greek tragedies to which the statement does not apply, there are Aeschylus' *Agamemnon* and *Prometheus.*

In the next chapter, Aristotle says that tragedies should be of "such length as will allow a sequence of events to result in a change from bad to good fortune or from good fortune to bad in accordance with what is probable or inevitable." [2] Again, Aeschylus' *Persians* and *Prometheus* do not support this suggestion, while *Oedipus Tyrannus* may be considered a, if not the, paradigm case.

In Chapter 8 Aristotle demands a tight unity of the plot.

---

2. In quotations from Aristotle's *Poetics* I have used the annotated translation by G. M. A. Grube: Aristotle, *On Poetry and Style,* The Library of Liberal Arts, Bobbs-Merrill, New York 1958. Scholars generally cite Aristotle by the traditional page numbers; but the chapter numbers furnished in the text above are also the same in all editions and less unwieldy.

Most of the other translations are my own, but I have consulted most of the standard translations.

Oedipus Tyrannus is the most extreme example, if not the only extant tragedy of Aeschylus or Sophocles, supporting it. A devoted admirer of Aeschylus could hardly have thought of any such demand, nor could any of Sophocles' other six tragedies have prompted it, except insofar as one might consider them inferior to *Oedipus Tyrannus* in this respect.

Finally, in Chapter 9 Aristotle stipulates that the plot should inspire pity and fear, and that this is "best achieved when the events are unexpectedly interconnected." Once more, there is no such unexpected interconnection in *The Persians,* in *Agamemnon,* in *Prometheus;* and there is little of it in some of Sophocles' other plays.

These passages in Chapters 6, 7, 8, and 9, in which *Oedipus* is not mentioned expressly, gain considerable weight when we find how often Aristotle mentions *Oedipus Tyrannus,* always approvingly and usually as a paradigm case. To this end, let us turn to Chapters 11 to 16.

2.

In the case of Chapter 11 of the *Poetics,* it will suffice to quote two sentences from Aristotle's discussion of reversal (*peripeteia*): "So in the *Oedipus* the man comes to cheer Oedipus and to rid him of his fear concerning his mother; then, by showing him who he is, he does the opposite. . . . The finest kind of recognition is accompanied by simultaneous reversals, as in the *Oedipus.*"

None of Aristotle's remarks about Oedipus are more interesting than those in Chapter 13, where the fateful notion of the tragic flaw or tragic error of judgment—*hamartia,* in Greek—is introduced. Aristotle considers four possible types of plots for tragedies.

First, we might be shown good persons going from happiness to misfortune; but this would never do, because it would simply be shocking. This is one of the points in the *Poetics* at which Aristotle's sensibility may seem shocking to us. But it is well to remember that Nahum Tate (1652–1715), who was an English poet laureate, rewrote the ending of *King Lear* in 1687 because Cordelia's death was widely felt to be intolerable: in his version Cordelia married Edgar. And Dr. Johnson approved heartily. We can also imagine a sensibility that—leaning on Aristotle, as we shall soon see—would not rewrite the play but find the ending tolerable only inasmuch as poor Cordelia was after all far from innocent, considering that her unrelenting stubbornness had brought about the tragic suffering of her father and, indirectly, her own death. But some of us find part of the greatness of this tragedy in its portrayal of a world in which the good may suffer hideously. And we shall see that in this respect Sophocles is at one with Shakespeare.

The *second* type of plot that Aristotle mentions briefly shows wicked persons who move from misfortune to happiness. Of this Aristotle says that it is the least tragic of all.

In the *third* type, we see a very bad person decline from happiness to misfortune. This, too, is far from tragic, Aristotle says, because we find it satisfying. In none of these three cases do we feel the two emotions that are part of Aristotle's definition of tragedy: pity and fear.

On the *fourth* type, let us quote his very words: "We are left with a character in between the other two; a man who is neither outstanding in virtue and righteousness, nor is it through wickedness and vice that he falls into misfortune, but through some *hamartia*.[3] He should also be famous or prosperous, like Oedipus. . ."

As I understand Aristotle, the fourth type, characterized by the celebrated tragic flaw or error of judgment, is reached

---

3. Grube has "flaw" at this point, as well as a footnote explaining that "a moral or intellectual weakness" is meant. He also discusses the concept on xxivf. and 10. To discuss the literature on *hamartia* at this point would lead us much too far afield.

by him at the crossroads of two lines of thought—and certainly not inductively, through a consideration of the masterpieces of Aeschylus, Sophocles, and Euripides. The first line of thought is *a priori:* there are said to be four possibilities; three are excluded, one by one; only the fourth remains. At no point does any consideration of various tragedies and their plots intervene. But Aristotle's thinking is by no means utterly abstract; he does not argue only through a process of exclusion, mindless of all evidence: he has known all along what model perfect tragedies have to approximate; and his ideal is, as usual, not laid up in the heavens but found in experience as the end of a development—in this case, Sophocles' play, *Oedipus Tyrannus.* Grammatically, to be sure, it would be possible that the character of the fourth or ideal type must be like Oedipus only by being famous or prosperous; but in context there can be no doubt that the whole description of this type reveals Aristotle's notion of King Oedipus. Before contesting this conception of the Sophoclean hero, let us still consider briefly three more passages from the *Poetics.*

In Chapter 14 we are told that the plot should inspire fear and pity, even if we do not see the play: "The story of Oedipus has this effect." And we might add: like few, if any, other tragic plots. But Aristotle does not tell us *why* it does. This is the riddle to whose solution I hope to contribute in the last part of this lecture.

In Chapter 15 Aristotle says that anything supernatural and inexplicable "should be outside the actual play, as in the *Oedipus* of Sophocles." And in Chapter 16 he remarks that "the best recognition" is "caused by probable means, as in the *Oedipus* of Sophocles. . ." It is plain that Aristotle means the *Oedipus Tyrannus* and not *Oedipus at Colonus* when he speaks of the *Oedipus* of Sophocles, and we shall follow his example from now on and simply speak of *Oedipus* when referring to the former play.

In sum, Aristotle's discussion concentrates very heavily on

the plot; particularly on the way in which the transition from prosperity to misfortune, or from misfortune to prosperity, is brought about. He is interested in the hero only incidentally, as the person who makes this transition in the course of the play.

3.

There is another reading of the play that is more popular than Aristotle's classical conception of *Oedipus* as the tragedy of "a man who neither is outstanding in virtue and righteousness" nor falls into misfortune "through wickedness and vice," but one who comes to a tragic end through a tragic flaw or error in judgment. The most widely accepted interpretation is that the play is a tragedy of fate. It is seen as a futile struggle to escape ineluctable destiny.

Obviously, there is some truth in this view; but it fails to distinguish between the Oedipus myth and Sophocles' plot, as we shall see later in detail. Moreover, if this really were the central theme of the play it would be difficult, if not impossible, to account for its tremendous impact from ancient to modern times, from Aristotle to Freud. After all, few if any readers or play-goers could have had any comparable experience of fate; and weird, extraordinary, far-fetched tales of things that are said to have happened once in dim antiquity to legendary people do not affect intelligent men and women the way this tragedy does.

It is the surpassing merit of Freud's interpretation of *Oedipus,* if we consider his comments merely as a contribution to literary criticism, that he brought out like no one before him how the tremendous impact of the story is connected with the way in which Oedipus is somehow representative of all men, including ourselves. *Mea res agitur.*

Interpreters have generally failed to distinguish this insight from the particular psychoanalytical exegesis offered by Freud. As a result, the classicists have failed to notice how Freud has gone beyond both Aristotle and the vulgar conception of the play as a tragedy of fate, advancing our understanding of *Oedipus* more than anyone else.

Freud's interpretation is stated briefly in the very first passage in which the Oedipus complex is explained by him—in a letter to Wilhelm Fliess, October 15, 1897. A little more than two years before the publication of the first and greatest of his major works, *The Interpretation of Dreams,* Freud writes his friend:

"The state of being in love with the mother and jealous of the father I have found in my case, too, and now consider this a universal phenomenon of early childhood . . . If that is so, one can understand the gripping power of *King Oedipus,* in spite of all the objections that the understanding raises against the assumption of fate—and one also understands why the drama of fate in later periods had to prove such a wretched failure. Against every arbitrary compulsion in an individual case our feelings rebel; but the Greek myth seizes upon a compulsion that everybody recognizes because he has sensed its existence in himself. Every member of the audience has once been potentially and in phantasy such an *Oedipus;* and confronted with the fulfilment of the dream in reality, everybody recoils in horror with the full charge of the repression that separates his infantile from his present state." [4]

In *The Interpretation of Dreams,* the same point is made in almost the same words, at slightly greater length. I shall quote this version only in part: [5] "If *King Oedipus* moves modern man as deeply as the contemporary Greeks, the solution must

---

4. Freud, *Aus den Anfängen der Psychoanalyse: Briefe an Wilhelm Fliess, Abhandlungen und Notizen aus den Jahren 1887–1902,* Imago Publishing Co., London 1950.
5. *Die Traumdeutung,* Franz Deuticke, Leipzig und Wien 1900, 181f. *Gesammelte Werke,* II/III, Imago, London 1942, 269.

surely be that the effect of the Greek tragedy does not rest on the opposition of fate and human will,[6] but must be sought in the specific character of the material in which this opposition is demonstrated. . . . His fate grips us only because it might have become ours as well, because the oracle before our birth pronounced the same curse over us as over him. Perhaps all of us were destined to direct our first sexual stirrings toward our mothers and the first hatred and violent wishes against our fathers. . .”

In the original edition of 1900, the discussion of *Oedipus* is immediately followed by one of the most remarkable footnotes in world literature. Here Freud shows in less than a page how his interpretation of *Oedipus* also illuminates *Hamlet*. It took eight years to sell the six hundred copies of the first edition of *Die Traumdeutung,* but eventually the book went through eight editions in Freud's lifetime.[7] In the later editions, this footnote is moved into the text, and followed by a new footnote which calls attention to the book in which Ernest Jones had meanwhile elaborated Freud's original note.

We shall take leave of Freud by quoting the end of the original note, preserved verbatim in the body of the text in the later editions: “Just as, incidentally, all neurotic symptoms —just as even dreams are capable of overinterpretation, and indeed demand nothing less than this before they can be fully understood, thus every genuine poetic creation, too, has pre-

---

6. Bernard Knox's *Oedipus at Thebes,* Yale University Press 1957, is one of the best modern studies of the play; and on the back cover of the revised paperback edition of 1966 the book is praised for being “aware of Freud.” *The Interpretation of Dreams* is indeed quoted at length on p. 4—in an old, notoriously unreliable, translation. As a result, Knox takes Freud for a champion of the view he in fact attacked—that “the *Oedipus Tyrannus* is a 'tragedy of fate,' [and] the hero's will is not free” (5)—in spite of the sentence to which the present note refers. Although even the translation he quotes got the meaning of *this* sentence right, Professor Knox was derailed by some mistranslations earlier on. Although he makes a point of the fact that Freud's “discussion of the *Oedipus* does not deserve the strictures which many classical scholars have wasted on it” (197), his own polemic also rests on a misunderstanding.
7. Ernest Jones, *The Life and Work of Sigmund Freud,* I, Basic Books, New York 1953, 360.

sumably issued from more than one motive and more than one
stimulus in the poet's soul and permits more than one interpretation."

Even if Freud's footnote consisted solely of this remark, it
would still be one of the most profound, suggestive, and en-
lightening footnotes of all time. If it should strike some readers
as mere common sense and obvious, they would do well to
keep in mind two striking facts. First, most popular versions
of Freud leave this insight entirely out of account—as if he
had thought that, for example, he had furnished *the* interpretation of *Hamlet*. But the footnote concludes: "What I have
attempted here is merely an interpretation of the deepest layer
of impulses in the soul of the creative poet." And secondly
the attempts at literary criticism by Freud's most popular
epigone, Erich Fromm, suffer greatly from the absence of this
insight. Yet they are meant to be, and they are very widely
considered, more commonsensical and less paradoxical than
Freud's interpretations.[8]

4.

The time has come to outline my own approach. Aristotle
largely omits consideration of the writer's conscious intent;
also of his historical context—either as a clue to his intent or
as a subject whose investigation might illuminate a tragedy.
This is not said in a carping spirit: rather the *Poetics* is so
interesting and has been so vastly influential, in spite of its
great brevity, that it is tempting to get lost in it, as if it were
impossible to go beyond it. Outside the Bible, there are not
many books of well under forty pages that have given rise to
such a huge secondary literature and to such intricate disputes
about the interpretation of the author's meaning in sentence

---

8. Erich Fromm, *The Forgotten Language*, Rinehart, New York 1951. For more
detailed discussion see my *Critique of Religion and Philosophy*, Harper, New York
1958; Doubleday Anchor Books 1961; section 77.

after sentence. When one considers that the impact of the book is largely due to the first sixteen chapters, while the discussion of diction in the last half is too closely tied to Greek words to merit comparable interest, one's admiration for the economy of a great genius who was able to say so much in so small a space—literally, less than twenty pages—is quite apt to lead one into reverend exegesis.

At this point it is well to recall that there is one whole dimension that Aristotle neglects: the writer's relation to his work. Besides the poet's conscious intent and the historical context of the work, we may add, thirdly, its biographical context. Thus nineteenth-century critics of Goethe's work, for example, paid attention not only to historical context but also to supposedly relevant incidents in his life and—taught by Goethe himself—to the history of his development (*Entwicklungsgeschichte,* in German). Goethe showed how his works could be illuminated by being considered in relation to each other, in their historical context and biographical sequence; and under his influence and that of Hegel, such developmental studies came to dominate the criticism of the nineteenth century. Another approach, developed in the twentieth century under Freud's influence, the psychological analysis of the writer and his works, may be assimilated under the same heading: biographical context.

There is yet another way of considering the artist's relation to his work, almost as alien to most criticism of the nineteenth and even the twentieth century as it is to Aristotle: we may choose to pay particular attention to an artist's experience of life.[9]

"Experience of life" is perhaps not self-explanatory. Many professors of literature do not scruple to speak of the writer's or artist's "philosophy." But this use of the word "philosophy"

9. See, e.g., my *From Shakespeare to Existentialism,* Beacon, Boston 1959; rev. ed., Doubleday Anchor Books 1960; especially Chapter 5 on Goethe and Chapters 12 and 13 on Nietzsche and Rilke.

is so remote from what most English-speaking philosophers today consider philosophy, and do when they "do philosophy," that it seems better to use another term. In another respect as well, "philosophy" would be more misleading than "experience of life": the former term is much too intellectual and bound to suggest that something systematic or at any rate conscious and deliberate is meant. But I do not have in mind a "philosophy" that an artist or writer has in the first place, and could express in straightforward, non-artistic propositions if he chose to, but elects instead to express indirectly in his work.

For all that, there is a sense in which Aristotle's approach to tragedy is not "philosophical" enough. Of his six formative elements—plot, character, thought, diction, melody, and spectacle—thought sounds as if it were relatively most philosophical; but what Aristotle means by thought is, as he plainly says, the thoughts the characters voice in their speeches. As it happens, the thoughts expressed in this way in some of the extant Greek tragedies are often of far greater philosophic interest than the speeches in most later dramas: *Antigone* and many of Euripides' plays come to mind as examples—but hardly *Oedipus.* Yet there is a sense in which *Oedipus* is philosophically very interesting.

5.

To get at the poet's experience of life, we must distinguish —as most discussions of *Oedipus,* for example, do not—between the myth and the poet's handling of it. In Shakespeare's case it is palpable that the stories he used are one thing and what he did with them quite another. The same point can be made more systematically in the case of the Orestes story: we can tell a great deal about the different experiences of life encountered in Homer, Aeschylus, Sophocles, Euripides, and Sartre by contrasting their handling of the same myth. Even more important is the fact that we cannot fully understand the works of the later poets unless we note their departures from earlier treatments. We cannot simply take Aeschylus' version for "the myth"; we must note how his story differs from Homer's—and Euripides' from both—and what variations Sophocles brings in—and how Sartre changes the old story. In the process, we realize how every one of these writers experienced life differently.[10]

In both Orestes' case and Oedipus' there is enough literary material for a bulky tome or a whole year's course in comparative literature. At least twelve Greek poets besides Sophocles wrote Oedipus tragedies that have not survived.[11] These twelve include Aeschylus, of whose Oedipus trilogy only the third play, *Seven Against Thebes,* survives (his *Laius,* his *Oedipus,* and his satyr play, *The Sphinx,* are lost), Euripides, and Meletus, one of Socrates' accusers. Among the Romans, Seneca wrote an Oedipus tragedy, and so did Julius Caesar,[12] who is also said to have dreamt that he had intercourse with his mother.[13] Among the French, Corneille returned to this theme (1659) soon after his own father's death; and at the age of 19, Voltaire wrote his first tragedy, on Oedipus (1718): here Jocasta never *loved* either Laius or Oedipus but only—a French touch—a third man, Philoctetes, and she was not happy with Oedipus. Later authors of Oedipus plays include Dryden and Lee and Hugo von Hofmannsthal. These facts may help to dislodge the stubborn presumption that Sophocles' Oedipus simply *is* Oedipus, that his plot is *the* plot.

It is of crucial importance methodologically to compare

10. See my article on "Nietzsche Between Homer and Sartre: Five Treatments of the Orestes Story," in *Revue Internationale de Philosophie,* 67, 1961, 50–73.
11. For their names see Otto Rank, *Das Inzest-Motiv in Dichtung und Sage,* Franz Deuticke, Leipzig und Wien 1912, 235. This book is much less well known in the English-speaking world than Ernest Jones' *Hamlet and Oedipus,* but its development and applications of Freud's ideas are incomparably more interesting.
12. Suetonius' Life of Julius Caesar, chapter 56.
13. *Ibid.,* chapter 7.

the poet's plot with *previous* treatments of the same material
in order to discover, if possible, his originality, his innovations,
and his own distinctive accents. In the case of Sophocles'
Oedipus we shall have to be satisfied with a few major points.

6.

The earliest versions of the Oedipus story known to us are
found in the *Iliad* and the *Odyssey,* and they differ markedly
from Sophocles' tale. The fuller account comprises ten lines in
the eleventh canto of the *Odyssey,* where Odysseus describes
his descent into the netherworld:

> *Then I saw Oedipus' mother, the beautiful Epicaste,*
> *whose great deed, committed unwittingly, it was to marry*
> *her own son who, having slain his own father, married*
> *her; and straightway the gods made it known among men.*
> *But he remained in dearest Thebes and ruled the Cadmeans,*
> *suffering sorrows in line with the deadly designs of the gods;*
> *while she descended beyond the strong bolted gates of Hades,*
> *plunging down in a noose from a lofty rafter,*
> *overpowered by grief; but for him she left infinite sufferings,*
> *forged by a mother's Furies (271–80).*

Here the true identity of Oedipus became known "straightway" [14] after his marriage, and there were presumably no
children; and while Jocasta (here called Episcate) hanged
herself, as in Sophocles' later version, Oedipus remained king
of Thebes, a man of sorrows.

The *Iliad* adds one further touch. In the twenty-third
canto, where the funeral games are described, one of the com-

---

14. On this point, that "straightway" is meant (as in the version in the Loeb
Classical Library, which I have consulted along with several other translations in
making my own), see W. H. Roscher, *Ausführliches Lexikon der griechischen und
römischen Mythologie,* Teubner, Leipzig 1897–1902, the long article on "Oedipus,"
701.

petitors is identified as the son of a man "who had come to Thebes for Oedipus' funeral, when he had fallen, and there had bested all the Cadmeans" (679–80). The implication is clear: after having reigned in Thebes for years, Oedipus eventually fell in battle and had a great funeral in Thebes, with games comparable to those described in the *Iliad* for Patroclus.

In Hesiod's extant works, the name of Oedipus occurs but once, in passing; [15] but among the fragments of the so-called "Catalogues of Women" we find three almost identical passages to the effect that "Hesiod says that when Oedipus had died at Thebes, Argeia, the daughter of Adrastus, came with others to the funeral of Oedipus." [16] All this is a far cry both from the conclusion of *Oedipus Tyrannus* and from *Oedipus at Colonus*.

Of the lost cyclic epics of the Greeks, the *Thebais* and *Oedipodia,* little is known. But in the latter it was Oedipus' second wife, Euryganeia, that became the mother of his children.[17] While this is consistent with Homer, the difference with Sophocles is striking. And in both epics, as also in Euripides' *Phoenician Women,* Oedipus merely retired in the end and did not go into exile.

Perhaps a few words that have survived as a quotation from the *Oedipodia* will go further than any lengthy argument toward exploding the common notion that Sophocles' story is *the* story, and that no distinction needs to be made between his plots and the ancient myths: the Sphinx "killed Haimon, the

---

15. *Works and Days,* 163: "at seven-gated Thebes, when they fought for the flocks of Oedipus." The reference might be to the battle in which, according to the *Iliad,* Oedipus fell.

16. Fragment 24 in *Hesiod, The Homeric Hymns and Homerica,* with an English translation by Hugh G. Evelyn-White, Loeb Classical Library, Harvard University Press, rev. ed. 1936, 172f.; cf. fragments 99A and 99. Adrastus is said to have been the only one of the "Seven Against Thebes" to have survived the attack on the city, and Argeia was Polyneices' wife.

17. Pausanias, IX.5.10: "Judging by Homer, I do not believe that Oedipus had children by Jocasta: his sons were born by Euryganeia, as the writer of the epic called *The Oedipodia* clearly shows" (*ibid.,* 482f.). See note 21 below for further discussion.

dear son of blameless Creon." [18] This should convince all who know Sophocles' *Antigone* how much freedom the poet enjoyed in using ancient traditions.

In Pindar we find a passing reference to "the wisdom of Oedipus" [19] as well as a passage about fate in which Oedipus is cited, though not by name, as an example:

> *His fated son encountered Laius*
> *and slew him, fulfilling the word*
> *given long before at Pytho.*[20]

Here we approximate the popular version of the story with its emphasis on fate.

Of Aeschylus' Oedipus trilogy we know only the third play, in which the theme of hereditary guilt is stressed: the sons pay for their father's sins, and there are stories of Laius' guilt. This appears to have been the thread that ran through the whole trilogy. And it *may* have been in Aeschylus that Oedipus' children were for the first time traced to his incest with his mother.[21]

Euripides' *Oedipus* has been lost, but in a fragment that has survived Oedipus is blinded by Laius' servants, not by himself. In his *Phoenician Women* the story is summarized once more in Jocasta's prologue (10ff.), and Oedipus' speech

---

18. Schol. on Euripides' *Phoenician Women,* 1750; *ibid.,* 482f.
19. *Pythian Odes,* IV, 263.
20. *Olympian Odes,* II, 38–40.
21. Roscher, *op. cit.,* 727, thinks so and cites *Seven Against Thebes,* 906 and 1015f.; see also 753f. Carl Robert, *Oedipus: Geschichte eines poetischen Stoffs im griechischen Altertum,* Weidmannsche Buchhandlung, Berlin 1915, I, 110f., argues that Euryganeia was not Oedipus' second wife but merely another name for Epicaste-Jocasta. In view of Pausanias' statement (see note 17 above) and Robert's admission that in the *Thebais* and *Oedipodia* Euryganeia apparently lived to see the mutual slaying of her sons (180f.), his argument seems unconvincing. R. C. Jebb, *Sophocles: The Plays and Fragments with Critical Notes, Commentary, and Translations in English Prose,* in the volume *The Oedipus Tyrannus,* Cambridge: At The University Press, 3rd ed., 1893, xv, ascribes "the earliest known version which ascribes issue to the marriage of Iocasta with Oedipus" to Pherecydes of Leros—who flourished about 456, a little later than Aeschylus. *Ibid.,* xvi: "Aeschylus, Sophocles and Euripides agree in a trait which does not belong to any extant version before theirs. Iocasta, not Euryganeia, is the mother of Eteocles and Polyneices, Antigone and Ismene."

near the end of the play adds a heavy emphasis on fate (1595 and 1608–14). But this play is later than Sophocles' *Oedipus,* and the surviving version embodies some fourth-century additions.

These comparisons permit us to grasp the tremendous originality of Sophocles' treatment. He might have moved the ineluctability of fate into the center of his plot, but he did not. Compressing the events of a lifetime into a few hours, he makes of Oedipus a seeker for the truth; and the conflicts in his tragedy are not the obvious ones but rather those between Oedipus who demands the truth and those who seem to him to thwart his search. Sophocles' Oedipus emerges as a magnificent, consistent, and fascinating character who is not taken over from the myths of the past but fashioned by the poet's genius.

The problem Sophocles moves into the center is how the truth about Oedipus finally came out. This is a point on which Homer and Pindar, Aeschylus and Euripides had said nothing; and the version in the *Oedipodia* was altogether different from Sophocles'.[22] Robert (62) surmises that the cruel piercing of the feet of Oedipus, when he was exposed, served no function whatever, except to provide, as it turned out, a sign of recognition: Oedipus must have arrived in Thebes with his feet and ankles covered, and Jocasta must have recognized him during one of the first nights. Robert believes that this was assumed in Homer; but few readers of the *Odyssey* would infer that it was Jocasta who recognized Oedipus. And the most important function of the piercing was surely to provide an explanation for Oedipus' name which, like his cult, antedated the story postulated by Robert. While "Swell-foot" is probably the right etymology, an altogether different origin of the name is very possible: one may think of the male organ— or of Immanuel Velikovsky's ingenious explanation in *Oedipus and Akhnaton: Myth and History* (1960), 55ff.

---

22. Roscher, *op. cit.,* 728.

In the many plays on the name in Sophocles' *Oedipus*,[23]
oideō (swell) does not figure, but *oida* (know) does, again
and again. While "Know-foot" is probably the wrong etymology, the story that Oedipus guessed the riddle of the Sphinx
and knew the feet probably represents another attempt to
explain his name. The riddle may have been old, but its injec-
tion into Oedipus' encounter with the Sphinx, no less than the
piercing of the feet, dates, if I am right, from the time after
Homer.[24] If so, two of the best known features of the myth
were introduced relatively late to explain the name "Oedipus."
And one of the motives for the post-Homeric blinding of Oedipus was probably to conform him to the riddle: we see him on
two feet, we are reminded of the helpless babe that could not
yet walk on two feet, and now we also behold him leaning on
a staff—on three feet, as the riddle put it.

In Sophocles' *Oedipus,* of course, all the motifs he adopts
from the myths are sublimated and spiritualized. And Sophocles' version of the recognition is evidently entirely original
with him.

I should like to add one personal observation before at-
tempting an interpretation. I have seen this play performed a
number of times: in a very small theater in Princeton, done
mainly by students; in Heidelberg, by professionals; in a large
theater in Princeton; a filmed performance in the Yeats translation, with masks; in Warsaw, with Stravinsky's music; and
in Vienna, in the Hölderlin translation, with music by Carl
Orff. This last performance was incomparably the best; but in
any version, however much there was that seemed objection-
able and imperfect in the staging or acting, the impact of the

23. See Knox, *op. cit.,* 182–84 and 264. But these are hardly, as he puts it, "puns";
for there is nothing funny about them; they are terrifying.
24. The earliest literary reference to the Sphinx is encountered in Hesiod's *Theog-
ony,* 326, where Oedipus is not mentioned any more than the riddle. Roscher,
op. cit., 715, notes that several scholars have pointed out that Herodotus evidently
did not yet know of any connection between the Sphinx and the Oedipus myth;
and Robert, *op. cit.,* Chapter 2, argues that in the original version of the myth
Oedipus killed the Sphinx without first guessing any riddle.

Sophoclean tragedy was overwhelming. At a personal level, then, the riddle of *Oedipus* means for me at least in part the question of why this tragedy should move me so incomparably. There was a time when I considered the *Antigone* a greater play and liked it better, wondering if *Oedipus* had not perhaps been overrated under Aristotle's influence. More and more, however, my *experience* of the play led me to feel that it was truly *non plus ultra,* the *Antigone* being one of the few trage-dies of all time that belong in the same class, along with *Aga-memnon* and the best of Shakespeare. What follows may be understood as an attempt to spell out why this tragedy is so effective.

7.

I want to call your attention to five central themes in *Oedipus Tyrannus,* without any claim that there are only five. They add up to a sketch of Sophocles' experience of life. To-ward that end they cannot be based on *Oedipus* alone. But to be sure that what I find in *Oedipus* is actually there instead of being merely a projection of the critic's own experience and ideas, one must ask in any case what other evidence there is that Sophocles himself felt as one thinks he did. Toward that end, too, we must read *Oedipus* against the background of the poet's other plays.

This does not mean that *Oedipus* must be approached as part of a trilogy: Sophocles did not write trilogies in the sense in which the *Oresteia* is a trilogy. While Aeschylus' trilogies often approximate a play in three acts, Sophocles merely of-fered three tragedies, one after the other—and both poets ended with a satyr play. But the plays Sophocles offered to-gether did not form a trilogy in the popular sense. Moreover, the *Antigone* was first performed about 442 B.C., *Oedipus Tyrannus* about 425 B.C. (the year is uncertain), and *Oedipus at Colonus* posthumously, having been finished in 406. Each of these plays was part of a different trilogy.

Sophocles was immensely popular, and 96 of his 120 plays won first prize (which means that he won twenty-four times, as each victory involved three tragedies and one satyr play); the others won second prize; he never placed third. But the year he offered *Oedipus Tyrannus* he won only second prize.[25]

That he occasionally returned to the same myths was not unusual but, on the contrary, a necessity, given the number of his plays and the amount of appropriate traditional material. Euripides, for example, wrote a fine *Electra* and an inferior *Orestes* that do not belong together: we know because both have survived. We also still have Euripides' *Trojan Women,* his *Hecuba,* his *Andromache,* and his *Helen,* each being an entirely independent play, and the characters that appear in several of these are sometimes drawn very differently. Instead of adducing further examples from Euripides, we might note that Odysseus in Sophocles' *Ajax* is quite different from Odysseus in the same poet's *Philoctetes.*[26]

In sum, before ascribing ideas to Sophocles we should pause to consider whether they find expression in more than one of his plays—and whether we can be sure the ideas were really his. With this in mind, let us interpret *Oedipus Tyrannus.*

8.

First of all, it is play about *man's radical insecurity.* Oedipus represents all of us. You might say: I am not like

---

25. He was defeated by Aeschylus' nephew, Philocles: see the article on Philocles in the *Oxford Classical Dictionary* (1949) and Jebb, *op. cit.,* xxx. Both fail to mention that his one hundred plays included a tragedy on Oedipus. This *is* mentioned by Rank, *op. cit.,* 235; but Rank fails to note Philocles' defeat of Sophocles' *Oedipus.*

26. If Roscher, *op. cit.,* 733, is right in suggesting that *Antigone,* 50ff. suggests that Oedipus died when he blinded himself, this would furnish an even more striking instance. Robert, I, 350, contests this interpretation. But at the very least these lines are incompatible with *Oedipus at Colonus* (cf. R. C. Jebb, *op. cit.,* the volume on *The Antigone,* 2d ed., 1891, 19, note for line 50).

him, my situation is different. But how can you know that? He thought his situation was different, too; and he was exceptionally intelligent and, like no one else, had guessed the Sphinx's riddle about the human condition. Indeed, he was "the first of men" (line 33).

In a play so full of ironies, can we be sure that Sophocles really conceived of Oedipus as "the first of men"? After all, Aristotle seems to have considered him an intermediate type, neither wicked and vicious nor outstanding in virtue and righteousness. And scholars have echoed this estimate through the ages. Thus Gilbert Norwood says in his book on *Greek Tragedy* that Oedipus "is the best-drawn character in Sophocles. Not specially virtuous, not specially wise. . ." [27]

We have seven of Sophocles' tragedies. Oedipus is the hero of two of them. What of Sophocles' other heroes? Were they middling characters, neither vicious nor outstanding? To begin with *Ajax,* the earliest of these plays, the last speech ends: "There never has been a man nobler than he." After that, the Chorus concludes:

> *Much may mortals learn by seeing;*
> *but before he sees it, none may*
> *know the future or his end.*

These themes are precisely those we find in Oedipus: the hero, far from being an intermediate character, is the noblest of men; but he falls suddenly and unexpectedly into utter misery and destruction; and this teaches us that none of us can be sure how we may end.

We never see Antigone prosperous and happy. Aristotle's canon notwithstanding, the action of the Antigone cannot be assimilated to any of his four types: she moves from utter misery to a heart-breaking but noble end. But she is certainly

---

27. Gilbert Norwood, *Greek Tragedy,* Hill and Wang (Dramabook), New York 1960, 149.

no middling character. Rather we may agree with Hegel who considered "the heavenly Antigone the most glorious figure ever to have appeared on earth." [28]

In *The Women of Trachis* Heracles is called "the noblest man who ever lived, whose peer you never shall behold again" (811f.). And a little later we are told again: "If any man counts on the morrow . . . he reckons rashly" (943ff.).

In the *Electra,* finally, it is similarly said of the heroine: "Was there ever one so noble. . . ?" (1080) Sophocles went out of his way to tell us quite explicitly that he wrote tragedies about the sufferings of exceptionally noble men and women. Like the author the Book of Job, he was far from believing that the best suffer least; he actually was at some pains to show that while less outstanding people tend to shun the extremes of suffering, like Ismene in *Antigone* and Chrysothemis in *Electra,* the noblest have a special affinity for the greatest suffering.

To return to *Oedipus Tyrannus,* it portrays, unlike the two plays just mentioned, the sudden and utterly unexpected fall from happiness and success of "the first of men." [29] In this it resembles Sophocles' *Ajax,* but the impact is incomparably greater and the play immensely superior in almost every way. One is reminded of Job and of *King Lear.* And there can be no doubt, in view of the seven extant plays, that man's radical insecurity formed part of Sophocles' experience of life.

9.

Secondly, *Oedipus* is a tragedy of *human blindness.* The immense irony of Oedipus' great curse (216ff.) consists in his blindness to his own identity. Later (371) he taunts Teiresias

---

28. *Vorlesungen über die Geschichte der Philosophie, Sämtliche Werke,* ed. Hermann Glockner, Frommann, Stuttgart, 1928, XVIII, 114.
29. Cf. Knox, *op. cit.*: "Oedipus is clearly a very great man" (50), and "Oedipus represents man's greatness" (51).

for being blind not only literally but also in his ears and spirit, although in fact Teiresias sees what Oedipus fails to see. And when Oedipus finally perceives his own condition, he blinds himself. That much is surely obvious.

Yet it is by no means merely his own identity that he is blind to; his blindness includes those he loves most: his wife and mother as well as his children and, of course, his father—their identity and his relation to them. It may seem that Oedipus' spiritual blindness, no less than his physical blindness at the end of the play, is peculiar to him and not universal. But the overwhelming effect of this tragedy is due in no small measure to the fact that Oedipus' blindness is representative of the human condition.

I have argued elsewhere that "the paradox of love is not that love should be commanded but that there is a sense in which it is hardest to love those whom we love most. To command people to put themselves into their fellows' places, thinking about the thoughts, feelings, and interests of others, makes excellent sense." [30] But even the wisest and most intelligent men who understand the human condition better than anyone else fail typically to comprehend those who are closest to them and whom they love most, because they are too involved with them emotionally. Oedipus, who solved the riddle of the Sphinx by perceiving that it portrayed the human condition and that the answer was "man"—Oedipus, who was "the first of men" and able to deliver Thebes from the Sphinx when even Teiresias, the seer and prophet, failed, comes to grief because he does not comprehend his relationship to those he loves most dearly.

Not only is this an aspect of the tragedy that Freud did not notice; in this respect Freud himself invites comparison with Oedipus. Ernest Jones argues in the last volume of his biog-

---

30. *The Faith of a Heretic,* Doubleday, Garden City 1961; Doubleday Anchor Books 1963, section 83.

raphy of Freud that Sandor Ferenczi and Otto Rank, who had
been personally closer to Freud than his other disciples, were
very sick men. This is surely interesting in a way not dreamt
of by Jones. He merely aims to show that their defection was
due to their lack of mental health; but another implication of
his evidence is rather more remarkable: the master who understood human psychology better than anyone else failed to perceive the psychological troubles of the disciples he loved most.
In this respect Freud, like Oedipus, was typical—and Oedipus
is even more representative of the human condition than Freud
thought.

We are overwhelmed by Oedipus' tragedy because, in the
words of Deuteronomy (19.20), we "hear and fear." It is
arguable whether "pity" and "fear" are indeed the two definitive tragic emotions, as Aristotle suggested; and one may at
the very least object to the English words, "pity" and "fear."

"Pity" is more than apt to suggest a measure of conde-
scension: we do not "pity" those to whom we look up. "Sympathy" may be a slightly better word, particularly if its literal
meaning is kept in mind: feeling with, suffering with. To be a
tragedy, a play must surely compel us to identify with those
who suffer and to feel their suffering as our own. And "fear"
sounds too petty and too specific: "terror" comes closer to
suggesting the feeling engendered by *Agamemnon* and *Prometheus, Oedipus* and *Lear*.[31]

If Oedipus' blindness were his peculiarity, as odd as his
fate seems to be, it would not terrify us. But we sense, however
dimly, that we ourselves are not too reliably at home with those
closest to us. The poet who deals with human relationships in
which almost all of his readers and his audience are involved,
too, has an obvious advantage at this point over writers who

---

31. "The exact meaning of *phobos* lies probably somewhere between fear and
terror" (Grube, *op. cit.*, 12).

portray exceptional relationships of which most men lack first-hand experience. No wonder, most of the greatest tragedies deal with the relation of lovers or that of parents to their children and children to their parents; and for sheer terror and sympathy and perpetual fascination no play ever written excels the *Oresteia* and *Oedipus, Hamlet* and *Lear;* and no novel, *The Brothers Karamazov* and *Anna Karenina.*

It would be idle to ask whether man's blindness, like his radical insecurity, is equally central in Sophocles' other tragedies. Plainly, it is not: Oedipus' eventual physical blindness sets him apart, and it is one of the *distinctive* characteristics of this play that it is the tragedy of human blindness.

That Creon, in the *Antigone,* fails to understand his son, Haimon—and for that matter also is far from foreseeing the suicide of his wife—provides no close parallel, because there is no presumption whatsoever in the first place that Creon is the wisest of men or singularly discerning regarding the human condition. On the contrary, it is plain from the start that he is not especially sensitive or perceptive. Ajax' blindness in his rage, just before Sophocles' tragedy begins, differs from Oedipus' in the same way. Sophocles' *Women of Trachis* is a little closer to *Oedipus* in this respect, for Deianira, Heracles' wife, is extraordinary in her generosity and empathy, and Heracles is elevated among the gods at the end; yet she kills him unwittingly, and he fails utterly to perceive her agony.

One psychological insight that is prominent in *Oedipus* is almost equally striking in *Antigone* and *The Women of Trachis:* that anger makes blind. Clearly, Sophocles was struck by the fact that a person whose anger is aroused will fail to understand what he is plainly told.

Yet anger does not account fully for Oedipus' blindness in the face of Teiresias' explicit accusations, and some readers may even feel that Oedipus is blameworthy at that point—or at the very least "that only once, confronted with the Sphinx, the hero's acuteness really stood the test, while in all other cases it goes astray." [32] However widely some such view is held, this strikes me as a serious misunderstanding. We do not do Oedipus justice, nor do we fathom Sophocles' profundity, until we realize how representative is Oedipus' failure. Whatever one may think of psychoanalysis, there would clearly be no need whatsoever for anything remotely like it, if those who are emotionally troubled could simply accept the truth as soon as they are told it.[33] But it is a common human experience that almost anyone can verify in a variety of striking cases that being told something is one thing, and being able to understand and accept it is another. And as long as one is not ready for it, one either fails to hear it, or does not get the point, or discounts it by discrediting the person who is speaking.

This experience is even more common than suggested so far: on re-reading a great novel or play, one frequently finds things that had escaped one the first time though they are plainly there. "Ripeness is all," [34] and until we are ready for an insight we are blind.

It is even conceivable that an interpreter of *Oedipus* today might find that the play says something rather plainly that previous exegetes have failed to notice for twenty-four centuries. But it would be ridiculous to blame this scholar or that for having been acute only once and for having gone astray the rest of the time. We should not identify with Creon of whom Carl Robert says that Wilamowitz was wrong in considering him a "self-righteous Pharisee," because in fact "he is fundamentally a comfortable Philistine by nature." [35]

Finally, it is worth noting how Aristotle, for all of his preoccupation with "recognition," stayed at the surface. He

---

32. Robert, *op. cit.,* I, 291.
33. Oddly, the claim that *"Oedipus* is, as it were, merely a tragic analysis [*eine tragische Analysis*]" is found in a letter Schiller wrote to Goethe, October 2, 1797.
34. *King Lear,* Act V, scene 2, line 11.
35. Robert, *op. cit.,* II, 102, and I, 285.

discusses this phenomenon as a part of stagecraft, as a device used in many tragedies, and most effectively in *Oedipus*. But he failed to see how recognition is in this tragedy not merely a matter of superb technique but of the very substance of the play, along with blindness.

10.

Thirdly, *Oedipus* is the tragedy of *the curse of honesty*. I shall not repeat here at length what I have developed elsewhere about the distinction between honesty and sincerity, and the importance of distinguishing degrees of honesty, even as we distinguish degrees of courage.[36] It is possible to be sincere, in the sense of believing what one says, while one yet has low standards of honesty: those with high standards of honesty take a great deal of trouble about determining the truth. They are not satisfied with the first belief at hand, adopting it sincerely; they question and persevere, even when others advise them to stop inquiring.

Oedipus, so far from being an intermediate character in Aristotle's sense—"not specially virtuous, not specially wise" [37] —is outstanding in his honesty. He is not only extraordinarily wise, possessed of more knowledge of the human condition than other men, and hence the only one who solved the riddle of the Sphinx; he is no less imposing in his relentless desire for knowledge and his willingness—nay, his insistence upon taking pains to find out what is true.

Modern readers, not versed in the classics, may feel that the attribution of such an ethos to a Sophoclean hero involves a glaring anachronism. But Sophocles' contemporary, Thucydides, formulated these standards in almost the very words

---

36. *The Faith of a Heretic*, sections 2 and 83.
37. Gilbert Norwood's phrase: see note 27 above.

I have used: "So averse to taking pains are most men in the
search for the truth, and so prone are they to turn to what lies
ready at hand." [38] Sophocles' Oedipus shares Thucydides' feeling, though not Thucydides' sarcastic contempt for oracles.[39]
This does not necessarily prove, as most writers on Sophocles
suppose, that the poet believed in oracles. He scarcely thought
that contemporary statesmen ought to be guided by them. After
all, the Athenians, including Aeschylus, had fought at Marathon in open defiance of the Delphic oracle, which had advised
the Greeks to yield to the Persians; and the greatness of Athens
dated from Marathon. But Oedipus belonged to the heroic age,
centuries earlier, and his story depended on his belief that the
oracle was probably right. This permits us no inference about
Sophocles' traditional piety.

Sophocles tells us how in Corinth, when a drunken man
had taunted Oedipus, suggesting that he was not the son of the
king of Corinth, Oedipus first questioned the king and queen,
who comforted him, and eventually pursued the question all
the way to Delphi. Typically, the oracle "sent me back again
balked of the knowledge I had come to seek," but informed
him instead that he was fated to lie with his mother and kill
his father—mentioning these two events in that order, not in
the sequence in which they were to be realized (779ff.).

More important, Sophocles constructs his whole plot
around Oedipus' relentless quest for truth, although the old
story was not a story about honesty at all. This is his most
striking departure from the mythical tradition. The central
spring of the action of Sophocles' tragedy is not, as it well
might have been, fate but rather Oedipus' imperious passion
for the truth.

The play begins with the priest's request that Oedipus save

---

38. I.20, conclusion; C. Foster Smith's translation in the Loeb Classical Library.
39. II.47 and 54, Thucydides comments sarcastically on oracles in connection with
the plague, and V.26 he speaks of "the solitary instance in which those who put
their faith in oracles were justified by the event." See also VII.50.

his city once more, from the plague this time; and Oedipus replies that the priest and the crowd behind him have not roused him like a sleeper: days ago, he has sent Creon to Delphi to determine "by what act or word I could save this city," and by now Oedipus is impatient for Creon's return because he cannot wait to know.

When Creon comes, he does not deliver a long speech to which Oedipus might listen patiently; rather Oedipus questions him searchingly and gradually extracts the oracle that the murderers (plural) of the late king Laius must be found and driven from the city. And soon Oedipus reproaches Creon for not having inquired more about the murder of king Laius when it happened, years ago. Burning with the desire to know, in spite of all obstacles, he has no sympathy for those who do not share this passion. He pronounces his great curse on all who know something about the murder and keep it silent—and, of course, on the murderer himself. There is no need for us to dwell here on the many ironies of that staggering speech.

Next, the Chorus suggests that Oedipus send for Teiresias, but again Oedipus has long sent for the prophet and is impatient because he is so slow to come. And when Teiresias does appear, he counsels Oedipus to stop inquiring because wisdom is terrible "when it brings no profit to the man that's wise" (316ff.). This attitude infuriates Oedipus: the prophet does not share his high standards of honesty but asks him outright to cease looking for the truth because it will not profit him. As if an Oedipus sought truth for his own profit!

Oedipus is not in the least concerned with his own happiness but in any case could not be happy knowing that his happiness hinged on self-deception. Moreover, he is deeply concerned with the welfare of his people for whom he, as king, is responsible: knowing that the plague will not cease until the murderer is found, Oedipus cannot give up the search merely because the seer thinks the truth would not profit him. Teiresias' attitude is, to his mind, preposterous:

> *You know of something but refuse to speak.*
> *Would you betray us and destroy the city?* (330f.)

More and more enraged by the prophet's refusal to tell what
he knows, Oedipus says, understandably:

> *If you had sight,*
> *I should have sworn you did the bloody deed alone* (348f.).

After all, how else could he explain Teiresias' stance?

When Teiresias flares up in anger at this taunt and, flatly
reversing his own stubbornly repeated vow of silence about
Laius' murder, shrieks, "you are the land's accursed defiler"
(353), Oedipus supposes that the old man no longer knows
what he is saying: he assumes that Teiresias, who has long
lost his respect, is simply cursing him. And when the old man
cries, "you are the murderer of the man whose murderer you
seek" (362f.), Oedipus thinks that he is merely shouting something, anything, to vent his impotent resentment and to cover
up the truth that he has long insisted on concealing. Soon,
therefore, he asks Teiresias whether Creon, who has also
seemed to drag his feet, albeit Laius was his sister's husband,
did not put the prophet up to his "design" (378f.).

All the conflicts in the tragedy are generated by the king's
quest for the truth. It would be pointless here to work our way
through every scene. Later, Jocasta counsels Oedipus to stop
inquiring, especially, but not only, in her last scene (1056ff.).
Again his persistence is testimony to his high standards of
honesty and to his concern for his people. The latter point is
worth mentioning because so many critics speak of his persistence as a fault, as if he could in decency accept Jocasta's
plea. But it is the former point that Sophocles keeps stressing.
Jocasta's pleas

> *If you have any care for your own life*
> *give up this search! My anguish is enough.* (1060f.)

and: *O be persuaded by me, I entreat you* [40]

---

40. This loving concern for Oedipus is "altogether different from the Epicaste of
the epic [the *Odyssey*, cited above], who conjures up the Erinyes against her son"
(Robert, *op. cit.*, 286).

meet with his unhesitating answer: "I will not be persuaded not to ascertain all this clearly" (1065).

Eventually, the shepherd, too, resists his pleas and literally begs Oedipus to ask no more; but Oedipus will not be put off. The issue is drawn clearly again and again: Oedipus is told by Teiresias, Jocasta, and the shepherd that self-deception and the refusal to face the truth may make a human being happier than his relentless honesty—and he spurns all such counsels as contemptible. And this is part of Oedipus' greatness and his claim to our awed admiration—precisely because it is *true* that honesty does not make the honest man happy.

To be sure, it is popular prattle that "honesty is the best policy," and even Plato preached the famous falsehood that virtue and happiness are one. But Sophocles' experience of life was more profound. For all his admiration of honesty, he knew how the man of surpassing honesty is alienated from all other men and driven to despair. In this respect, too, Oedipus is representative of the human condition.

Are we reading our own experience of life into *Oedipus,* imputing to Sophocles concerns that were quite alien to him? Or do any of his other tragedies suggest that the curse of honesty was part of his experience of life? In the *Philoctetes,* too, honesty does not figure in the traditional myth, but Sophocles' whole tragedy is built around Neoptolemus' high standards of honesty, and nobody could possibly doubt the poet's admiration for this virtue. Nevertheless, Neoptolemus' honesty makes for a tragic conclusion, which in this play is averted at the last moment by a *deus ex machina.* Thus we need not fear that we have merely projected the curse of honesty into Sophocles' experience of life.

11.

Fourthly, *Oedipus* is a play about a tragic situation—a drama that shows how some situations are characterized by *the inevitability of tragedy.* If Oedipus gave up his quest, he would fail his people, and they would continue to die like flies: his honesty benefits them, but at the cost of destroying not only him but also Jocasta and the happiness of their children. Whatever he does in the situation in which Sophocles places him at the beginning of the play, he incurs a terrible guilt. Again, this is Sophocles' genius and not in any way dictated by the myth. And in this respect, too, Sophocles' Oedipus is representative of the human condition.

Most interpreters quite fail to see this dilemma, and many readers suppose that Oedipus, of course, ought to take the advice he is given and desist from his search. In his third treatment of the play, in *Poiesis* (1966), H. D. F. Kitto derides any notion that we are shown an "ideal King who will properly and nobly do his duty by doing his utmost to deliver the city from peril, even at the cost of his own life—an interpretation which . . . founders on the simple fact that it never occurred to Sophocles to mention that the city in fact was delivered. Naturally, we could infer it, but if we are really attending to the play, we shall not even think of it." [41]

Here Kitto, often so suggestive and always a pleasure to read, is surely unconvincing. In the first place, an interpretation of Oedipus' motivation obviously could not founder even on the fact that the oracle subsequently did not keep its solemn promise and allowed the plague to continue after the murderer of Laius had been driven from the city; much less on the fact that Sophocles' tragedy ends before Oedipus is driven from the city, and we are told plainly that Creon is seeking further instructions from Delphi. Secondly, if we really attend to the play we should realize that Oedipus' anger at

---

41. *Poiesis: Structure and Thought* (Sather Classical Lectures: Volume 36), University of California Press, Berkeley and Los Angeles 1966, 209. Cf. Kitto's *Form and Meaning in Drama,* Methuen, London 1956, University Paperbacks 1960, 200. Kitto also had a section on this play in his *Greek Tragedy* (1939); rev. ed., Doubleday Anchor Books (n.d.), 142ff.

Teiresias and Creon is prompted in large measure by their lack of concern for the city. We have already quoted Oedipus' words to Teiresias:

> *You know of something but refuse to speak.*
> *Would you betray us and destroy the city?* (330f.)

And we should also note that when Teiresias mocks Oedipus, saying that his very greatness has proved his bane, the king replies:

> *I do not care if it has saved this city* (442f.).

Finally, Kitto notes: so much is made of the plague in the beginning, and then "Oedipus or Creon mention it (at vv. 270–272, 327, 333, 515f.); so too does Iocasta, at her first entry (vv. 635f.). Thereafter it is totally forgotten." [42] And others have suggested that the plague is simply taken over from the beginning of the *Iliad*. But there was surely no chance for the plague to be totally forgotten by the audience, let alone for them to consider it a mere literary allusion. Athens had been devastated by the plague only a few years earlier, in 430 and in 429, when her first citizen, Pericles, died of it along with a very large part of the population; and this had proved a turning point of the Peloponnesian War, which was still raging and, of course, eventually lost by Athens. Pericles was a statesman of extraordinary wisdom, but the plague upset his calculations and took his life. There were probably few in the audience who had not lost members of their families and close friends to the plague, and few who did not feel reminded of Pericles. The vivid description of the plague in the beginning must have struck terror into their hearts. And what other crucial elements in the story are given more space? Oedipus' obligation to do all he can to save the city must have been very clear to the audience.

---

42. *Ibid.,* 209.

To be sure, most men never find themselves in situations in which tragedy is as dramatically inevitable, whatever they do, as it is for Oedipus, Antigone, and Neoptolemus. Still, millions have found themselves in situations in which they either had to incur the guilt of breaking the law and suffering a cruel death (like Antigone) or had to continue to live with the knowledge that they had abetted some moral outrage. And it is far from being an uncommon experience that *raison d'état,* or at any rate the interest of some major enterprise and the welfare of a lot of people, dictates dishonesty (the course Odysseus would embrace in *Philoctetes*), while the man who values honesty (like Neoptolemus) must choose between incurring the guilt of dishonesty or shouldering the blame for wrecking some great undertaking. In *Oedipus* the welfare of the people requires honesty—and a tragic self-sacrifice.

More generally, it is a chronic feature of the human condition that we cannot please and benefit all, any more than Oedipus can; we cannot satisfy all the claims that we should meet. Sartre has said, speaking of "The Responsibility of The Writer":

"If a writer has chosen to be silent on one aspect of the world, we have the right to ask him: Why have you spoken of this rather than that? And since you speak in order to make a change, since there is no other way you can speak, why do you want to change this rather than that?" [43]

Alas, the "if" is unwarranted: none of us can speak about all aspects of the world or press for all the changes that would benefit our fellow men. Those who press for a great many changes can always be asked both: why do you work for all of these but not for those? and: why are you scattering your energies instead of concentrating on one major effort? There is no way out. Luther realized this and insisted that in a life

---

43. "The Responsibility of the Writer" (lecture at the Sorbonne, in 1946, at the first general meeting of UNESCO) in *The Creative Vision: Modern European Writers on Their Art,* ed. H. M. Block and H. Salinger, Grove Press, New York 1960.

devoted to works failure was inevitable, but he believed in salvation through faith in Christ's vicarious atonement and in eternal bliss after death. Sophocles' experience of life was different.

12.

Fifthly and finally, *Oedipus* is a play about *justice*. Indeed, it calls justice into question in two ways and at two levels. First, we are all but compelled to ask ourselves whether Oedipus' and Jocasta's destruction is just. Do they deserve what happens to them? The answer can hardly be in doubt: they don't. We may concede that both have their faults—as who does not?—and yet insist that they get worse than they deserve; incomparably worse, like Antigone and Lear. Indeed, Oedipus' faults are closely related to his passion for honesty and his intolerance of dishonesty. His faults are inseparable from his righteous—should we say, "just"?—indignation.

In fact, he did not really "murder" king Laius, his father. The act was wholly unpremeditated, prompted in equal shares by self-defense and righteous indignation: the charioteer hit Oedipus who, in return, struck him;

> *When the old man saw this, he waited for the moment*
> *when I passed, and from his carriage he brought down*
> *full on my head, his double-pointed goad.*

Oedipus hit back and killed him with one stroke (800ff.).

At the first level, then, the tragedy raises the question of the injustice of men's fates and their sufferings. The nobler often—if not more often than not—fare worse than those who are less admirable.

Justice, however, is also called into question in another way. Even as Sophocles, for all his admiration for honesty and his palpable disapproval of Odysseus' ethic in *Philoctetes*, perceives the curse of honesty, he also calls into question *human* justice. To be sure, he does not do this after the man-

ner of Thrasymachus or Callicles in Plato's *Republic* and
Gorgias; nor does he do it as a philosopher might. The poet's
communication is, to use Kierkegaard's term, "indirect." For
all that, it is more powerful if we measure its impact on those
who get the point; only most readers, play-goers, and critics
do not get the point—consciously. This does not rule out the
possibility that the tragedy strikes terror into hearts that dimly
sense how their most confidently championed moral values are
shown to be extremely problematic.

Who can hear Oedipus' great curse (216ff.) without feeling this? Sophocles does not argue and plead, saying, as it
were: look here, a murderer is a human being, too; and there,
but for the grace of God, go you and I. He offers no comment
and does not need to because the audience knows that the
murderer on whom the king pronounces his curse is none
other than the king himself. Were that not so, few men before
the nineteenth century would have seen grounds to question
that the curse was just, if stern. But if that is justice, should
we not be better off without it?

The king's desire, just a little later, to punish Teiresias
and Creon might be called unjust. But given the facts as they
appear to Oedipus, would not the punishment be just? And is
not this another way of questioning man's justice—to remind
us how the facts are easily misunderstood, and how punish-
ments that to the righteously indignant seem to be unquestion-
ably just are often anything but that?

Yet later, Jocasta kills herself. And Oedipus blinds himself
and insists on being exiled. These self-punishments, too, are
acts of human justice and quite problematic.

The poet does not offer us alternative solutions. But the
dark side of justice is exposed more powerfully than perhaps
by any one before his time. We usually assume that justice is
unproblematically good. Sophocles shows us how questionable
it is; and this, too, is part of the greatness of the tragedy and
of its powerful effect.

13.

In the end, let us consider *Oedipus* in the light of some of Plato's remarks about tragedy. In the *Republic* Plato offers three sweeping generalizations that are simply wrong when applied to this play.

"Strip what the poet has to say of its poetic coloring, and you must have seen what it comes to in plain prose. It is like a face that was never really handsome, when it has lost the fresh bloom of youth" (601).[44]

That is beautifully put and true of most literature—especially literature with some philosophical pretensions. But I have tried to show how utterly false it is in the case of Sophocles. And an Athenian philosopher who was over twenty when Sophocles died—and Sophocles wrote till the end—might have taken Sophocles into consideration when he discussed tragedy. Yet Plato never once quotes Sophocles, and he mentions him only twice—once in the *Republic* (329B), on an anecdotal, sub-literary level.

Plato's second generalization is that the poets do merely what pleases the multitude and reproduce conventional opinions.[45] Again, this is no doubt true of the great majority. But I have tried to show that it is false about Sophocles.

Thirdly, poetry is, according to the *Republic* mere imitation of appearances; it turns our attention in the wrong direction, while mathematics, being incomparably closer to philosophy, leads the soul to face in the right direction, toward universals that are not ephemeral and do not change (509ff., 597–608). This view of literature is hardly very perceptive and utterly misses the philosophical import of Sophocles.

These criticisms of Plato are not unfair, considering his

---

44. F. M. Cornford's translation, Oxford University Press 1945.
45. *Republic* 602 and 479 D; cf. Cornford, *op. cit.,* p. 333, note 1.

resolve to banish from his commonwealth not only tragic poets of inferior worth but tragic poets generally. It was surely incumbent on a philosopher taking that stand at that historical moment to consider Aeschylus, Sophocles, and Euripides no less than their epigones of the fourth century.

Next, let us compare Plato's explicit prescriptions for the poets with Sophocles' practice. According to Plato, the poets must insist that the divine is responsible for good only, never for evil, and that the divine never deceives (379ff.). *Oedipus*, like the Book of Job, is more realistic.

Plato insists that virtue must be rewarded in literature—a point repeated in *The Laws* (663)—and that goodness must be shown to be more pleasant. Surely, Sophocles was more profound.

And in *The Laws* (660) Plato would compel the poets to write only about men "in every way good." One can see how Aristotle's views, which I have criticized in the beginning, represent some slight improvements over Plato's notions; but one should add, as Aristotle's admirers through the ages have not done, that though he may be less wrong than Plato, there is no reason for applying altogether different standards to the two philosophers, as far as their ideas about tragedy are concerned. It has been the fashion to dismiss Plato's ideas on the subject very lightly, while assuming that Aristotle must very probably be right in the main. It seems more reasonable to suggest that he made partial but insufficient amends for some of Plato's errors.

14.

Sophocles surely meant to teach humility—by reminding us, for example, of man's insecurity and blindness. We may contrast this with Plato's overconfidence in himself and in his rational vision.

Sophocles further differs from Plato in showing us that virtue and happiness are not Siamese twins. And he realized that some of the virtues are profoundly problematic. Plato, on the other hand, believed in the compatibility of all the virtues and in the desirability of making everybody as virtuous as possible.

If we closed on this reflection, we should give a misleading picture of both men. These points were worth making because they help to show Sophocles' philosophical relevance by suggesting that he was right on matters of profound importance on which Plato was wrong. But the note on which I wish to end involves a final *peripeteia,* a reversal.

Sophocles did not strike his contemporaries the way he strikes me. Incredible as it may seem, his tragedies—even *Oedipus*—apparently had a somewhat sedative effect: the audience felt that it learned moderation, accommodation, resignation. Sophocles celebrates the hero who goes to the opposite extremes; but the audience is much more likely to conclude that it is wise to lie low.

This may help to explain Sophocles' reputation for piety, and it also provides some content for one of the most celebrated conceptions in Aristotle's *Poetics: catharsis.* Whatever Aristotle may have meant—and the literature on that question is staggering—he clearly disagreed with Plato's claim that the exhibition of violent emotions on the stage is likely to lead men to emulate, say, a Philoctetes (the example, of course, is mine) by shrieking and moaning in agony instead of learning self-mastery. Aristotle suggested that emotional people, particularly the less educated, need some relief and purgation— precisely in order to behave with more restraint in real life.[46] What neither Plato nor Aristotle realized was that most men's

---

46. Cf. the final chapter of Aristotle's *Politics* (VIII.7) and Grube's discussion, *op. cit.,* xvff. For two other suggestions about catharsis, see my "Nietzsche between Homer and Sartre" (note 10 above), 60 and 72.

daring is so slight that it can be spent in an hour's identification with *Oedipus* or *Antigone;* then their spirit, having taken its brief flight, settles down again on the level of Antigone's sister, Ismene, or Electra's sister, Chrysothemis, or Oedipus' foil, Creon. In that sense, Sophocles became a teacher of traditional piety.

Plato, on the other hand, set up societies, both in *The Republic* and in *The Laws,* in which moderation, accommodation, and temperance are held high as norms and Sophoclean tragedies are not allowed. But many readers are much more deeply affected by Plato's own refusal to resign himself, to accommodate himself, to be moderate—by his radicalism—by his Oedipean spirit. And it may take a reader trained by Plato—a philosopher—to read *Oedipus Tyrannus* as I have done.